THE ZOMBIE Doodle Diaries

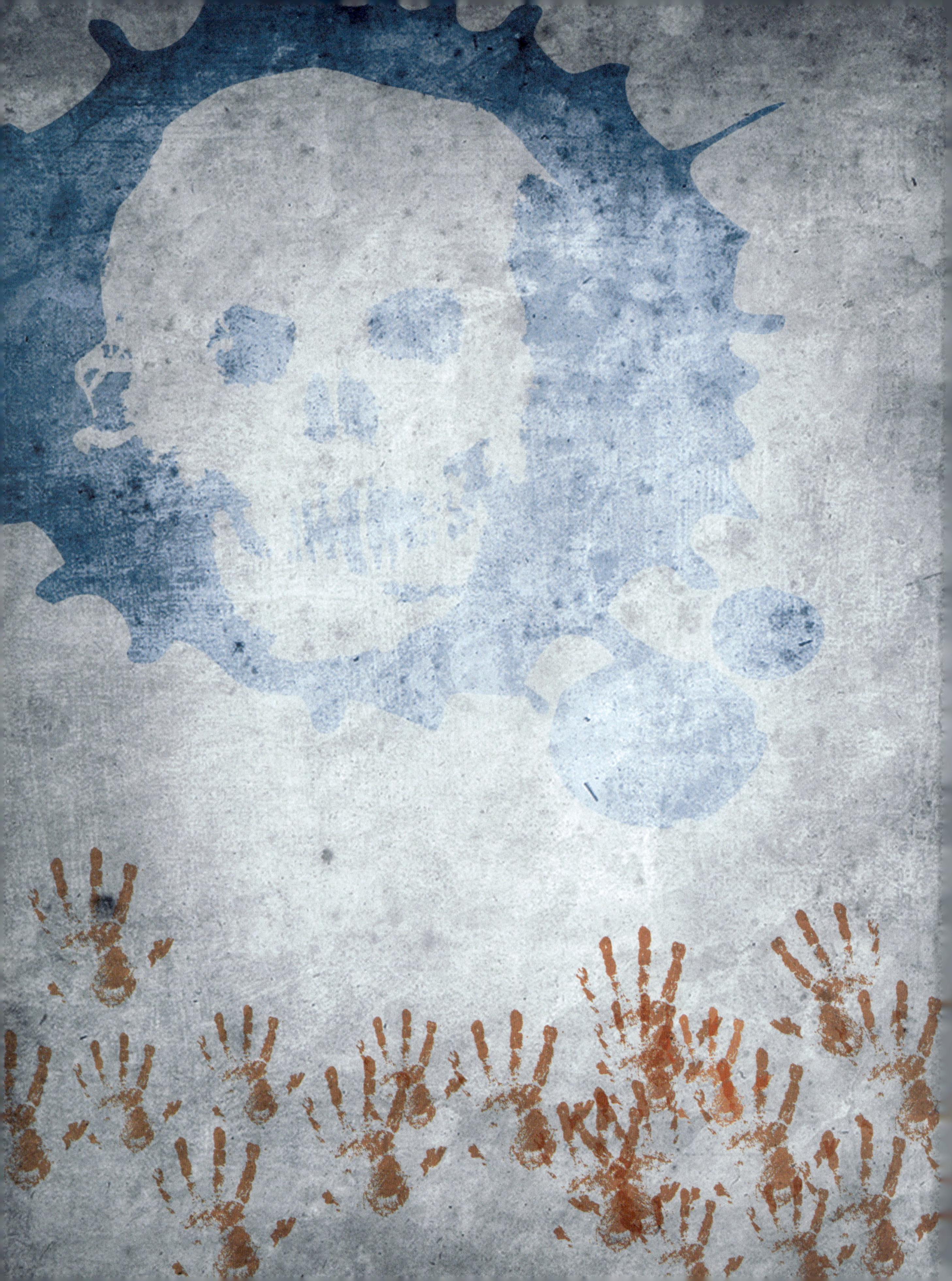

The Zombie Doodle Diaries

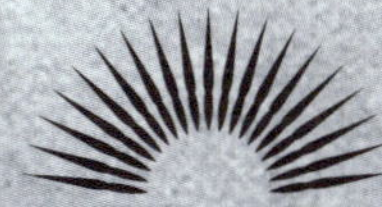

THUNDER BAY
P·R·E·S·S
SAN DIEGO, CALIFORNIA

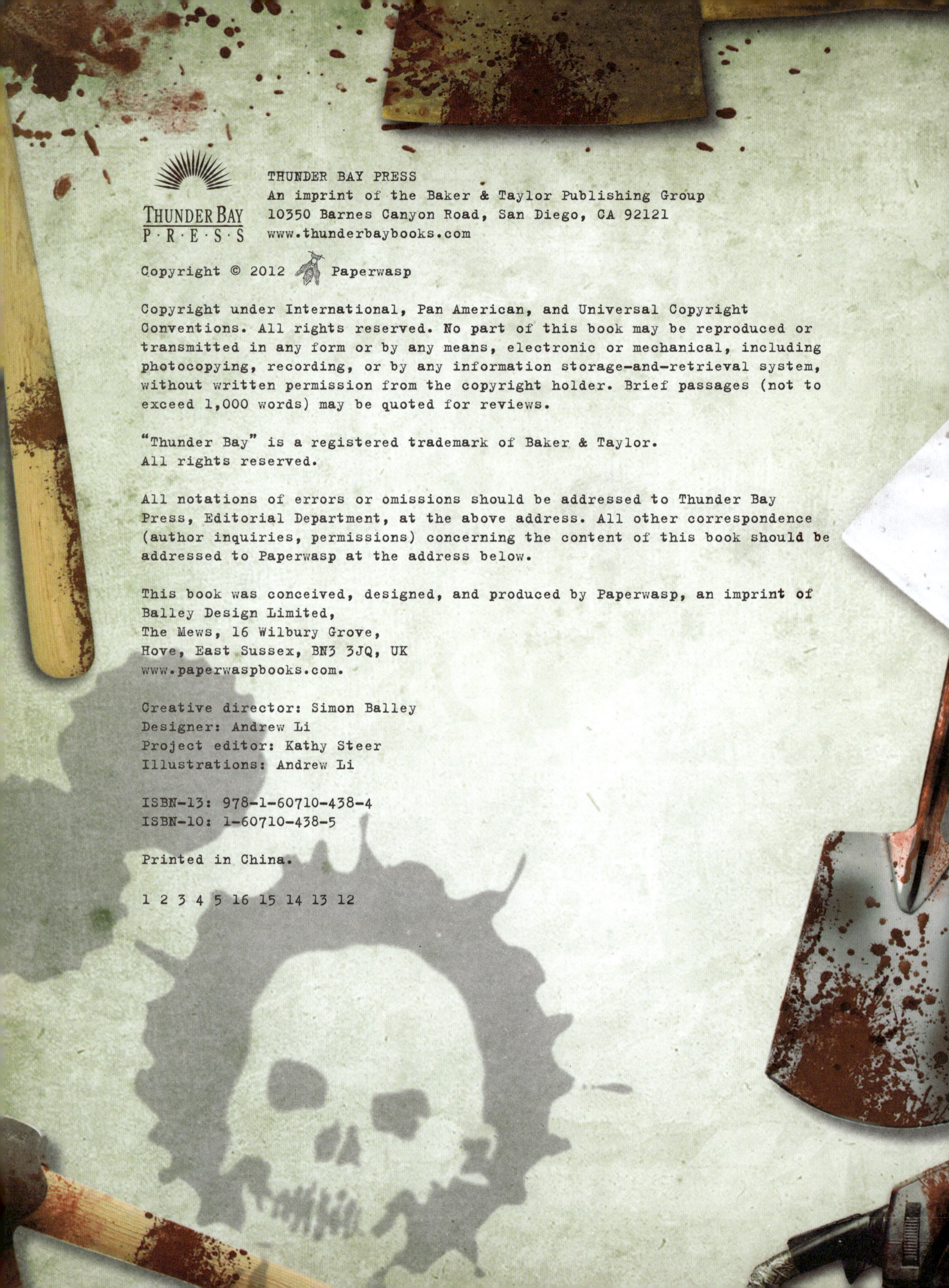

THUNDER BAY
P·R·E·S·S

THUNDER BAY PRESS
An imprint of the Baker & Taylor Publishing Group
10350 Barnes Canyon Road, San Diego, CA 92121
www.thunderbaybooks.com

All notations of errors or omissions should be addressed to Thunder Bay Press, Editorial Department, at the above address. All other correspondence (author inquiries, permissions) concerning the content of this book should be addressed to Paperwasp at the address below.

This book was conceived, designed, and produced by Paperwasp, an imprint of Balley Design Limited,
The Mews, 16 Wilbury Grove,
Hove, East Sussex, BN3 3JQ, UK
www.paperwaspbooks.com.

Creative director: Simon Balley
Designer: Andrew Li
Project editor: Kathy Steer
Illustrations: Andrew Li

ISBN-13: 978-1-60710-438-4
ISBN-10: 1-60710-438-5

Printed in China.

1 2 3 4 5 16 15 14 13 12

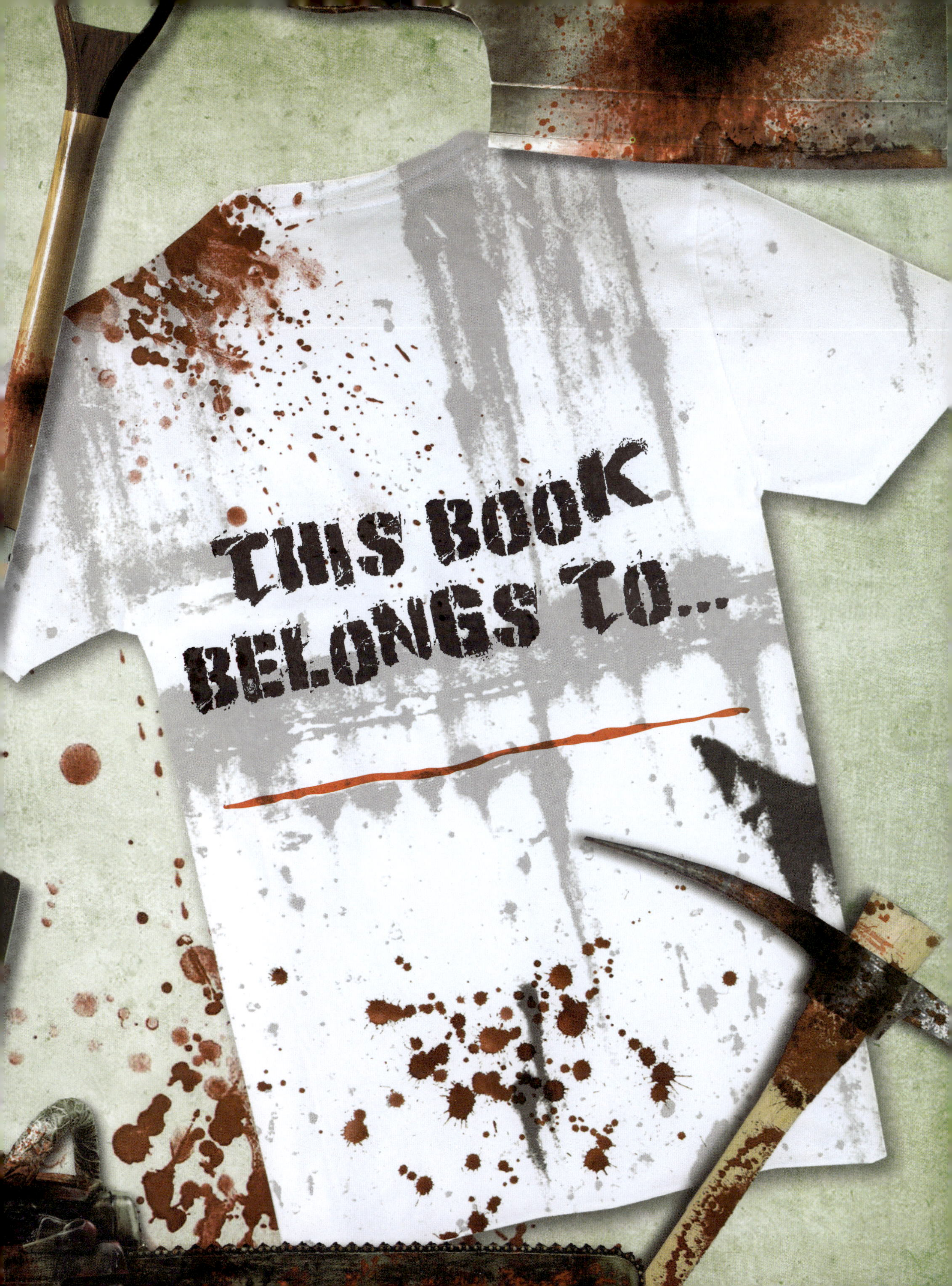
THIS BOOK
BELONGS TO...

Zombie Family Tree

Write your family members' names here.

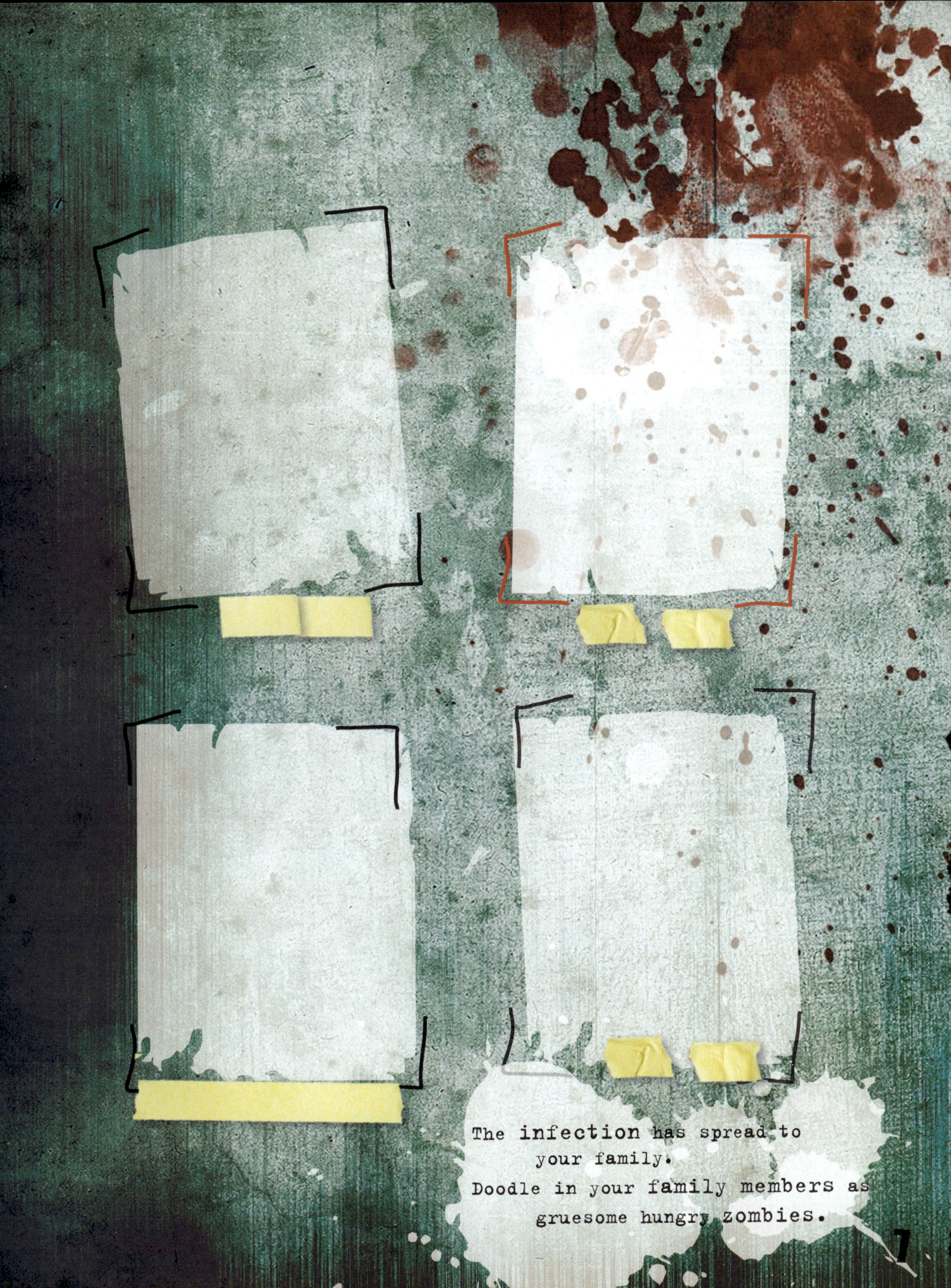
The infection has spread to
your family.
Doodle in your family members as
gruesome hungry zombies.

WORD SEARCH 1

B I T E E B E G I V S

S I C K I L S O E I D

E N T G H O R R O R E

T F K R B O N E S U A

G E G U B D E V Z S D

O C E E R S P O O K Y

U T L S A D O L M U I

D I B O I E G T B L I

H O E M N A R I I L Z

I N T E S T I N E S R

G R A V E H M G U T S

bite
blood
bones
brains
dead
death
horror

infection
intestines
grave
grim
gore
gruesome
guts

revolting
sick
skulls
spooky
virus
zombie

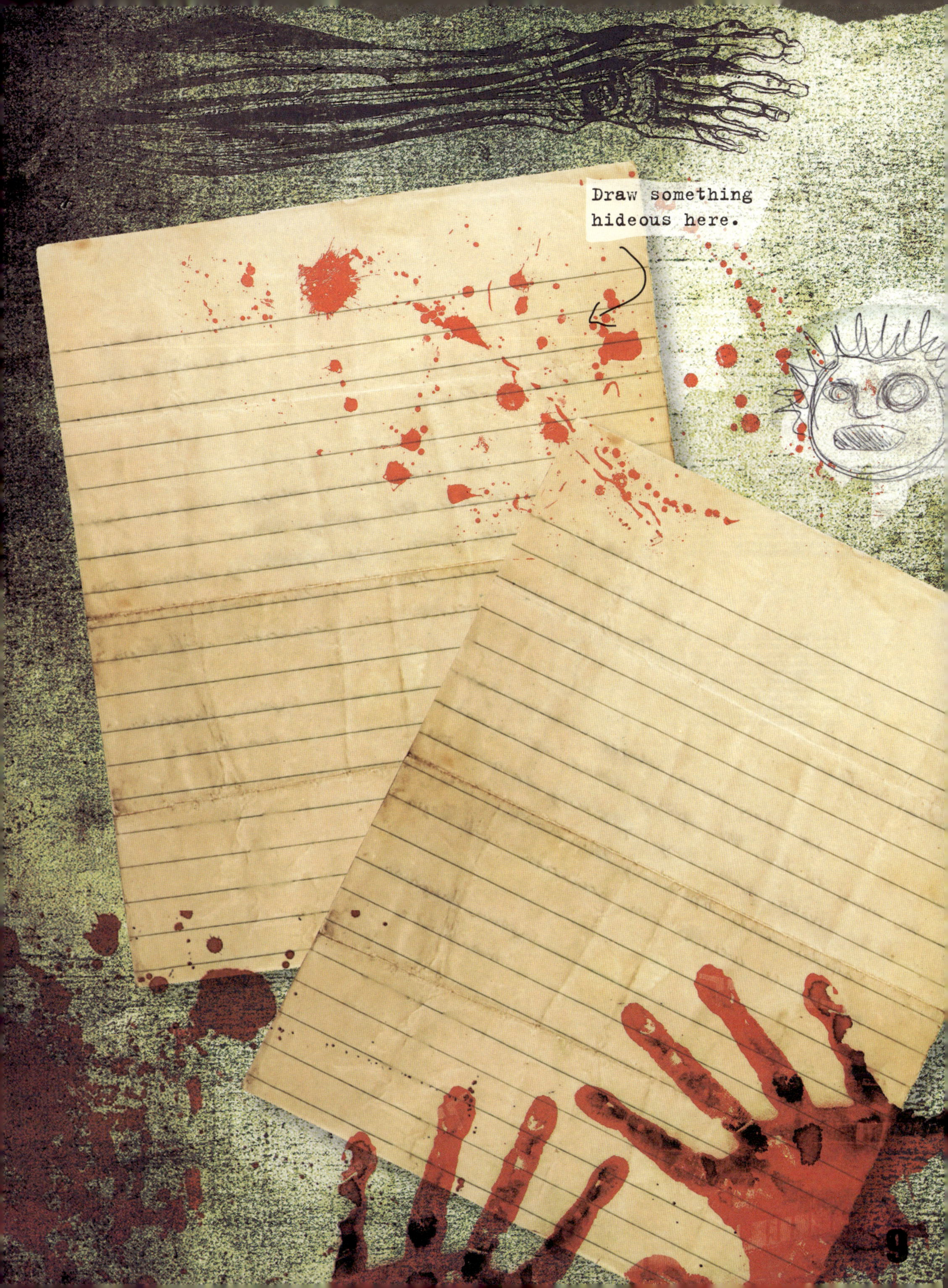
Draw something
hideous here.

LIFELINES

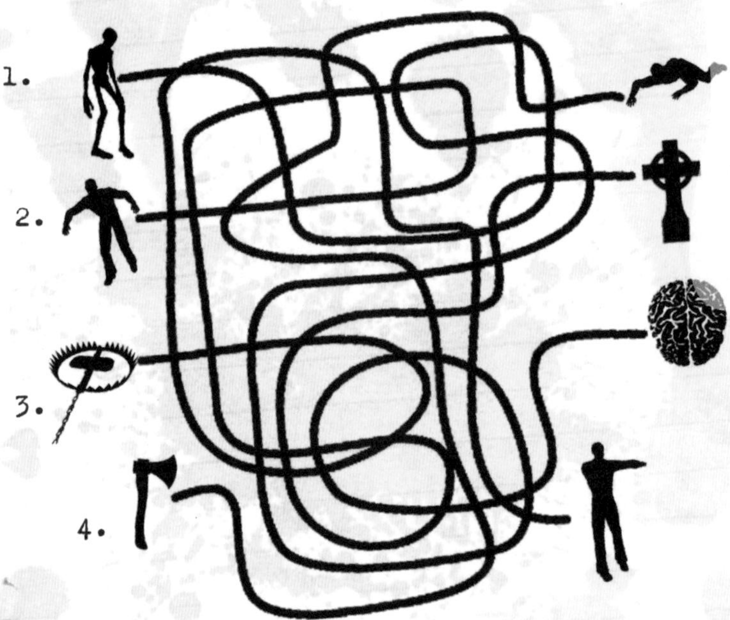

1. What does the skinny zombie finally feed on?
2. Where does the sleepy zombie decide to rest?
3. Find which zombie has escaped the trap?
4. Discover which zombie gets the axe?

ZOMBIES MAKE GREAT PETS; THEY ALREADY KNOW HOW TO PLAY DEAD

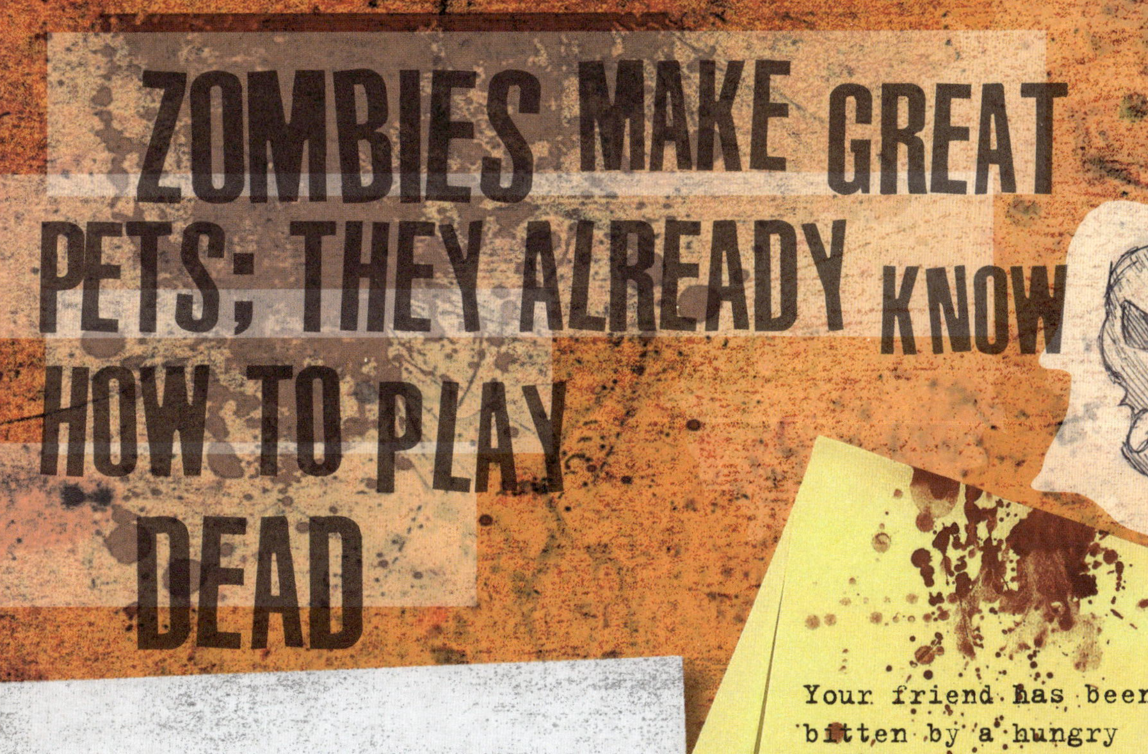

Your friend has been bitten by a hungry zombie. Write their obituary here.

ZOMBIE HANGMAN

Cross off the dead letters.

ABCDEFGHIJKLMNOPQRSTUVWXYZ

Draw your hangman.

Enter your blood-soaked words here.

ABCDEFG HIJKLM NOPQRST UVWXYZ

Cross off the dead letters.

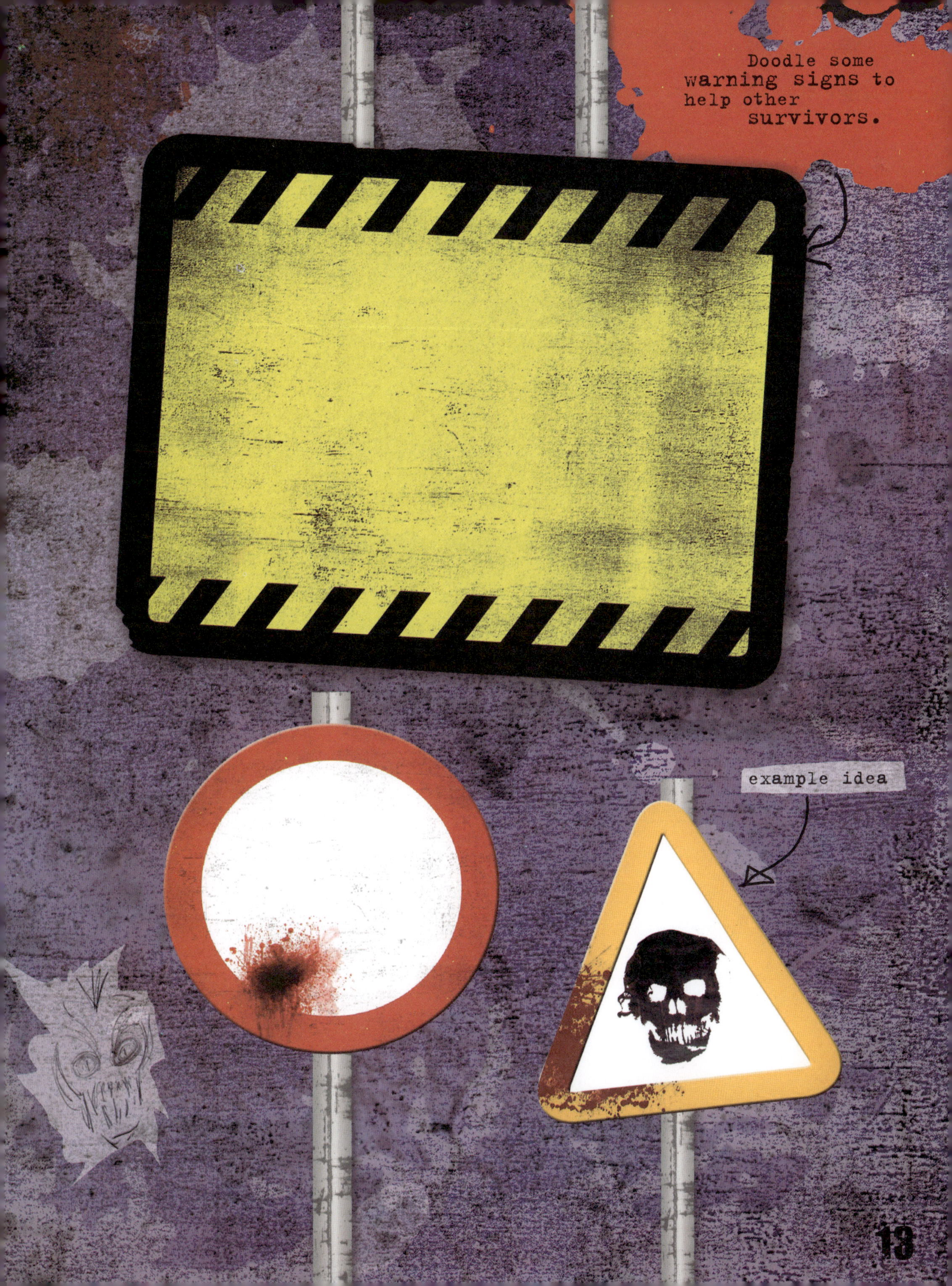
Doodle some
warning signs to
help other
survivors.
example idea

Connect the ~~Zombies~~ Dots

...and reveal something even more evil!

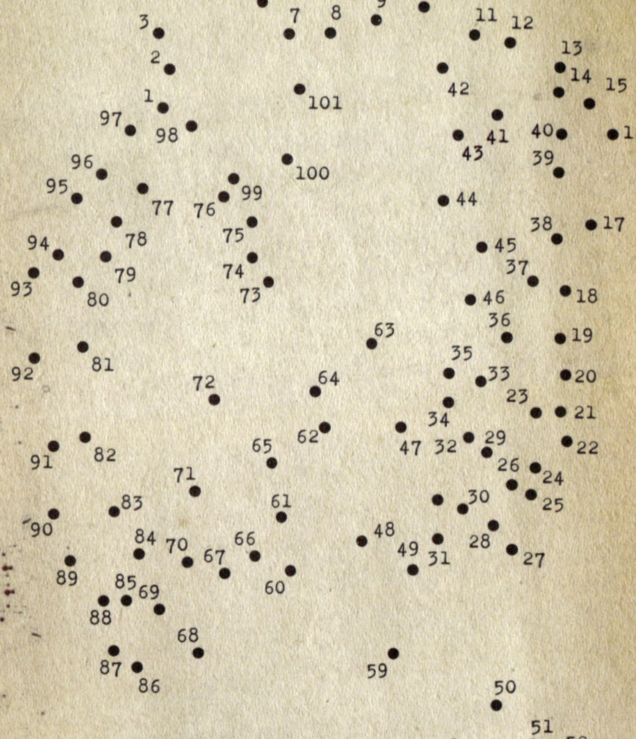

Zombies originally hail from Haiti. Voodoo sorcerers (or bokors) from the Caribbean are believed to be able to revive the dead with magic potions, powders, and incantations.

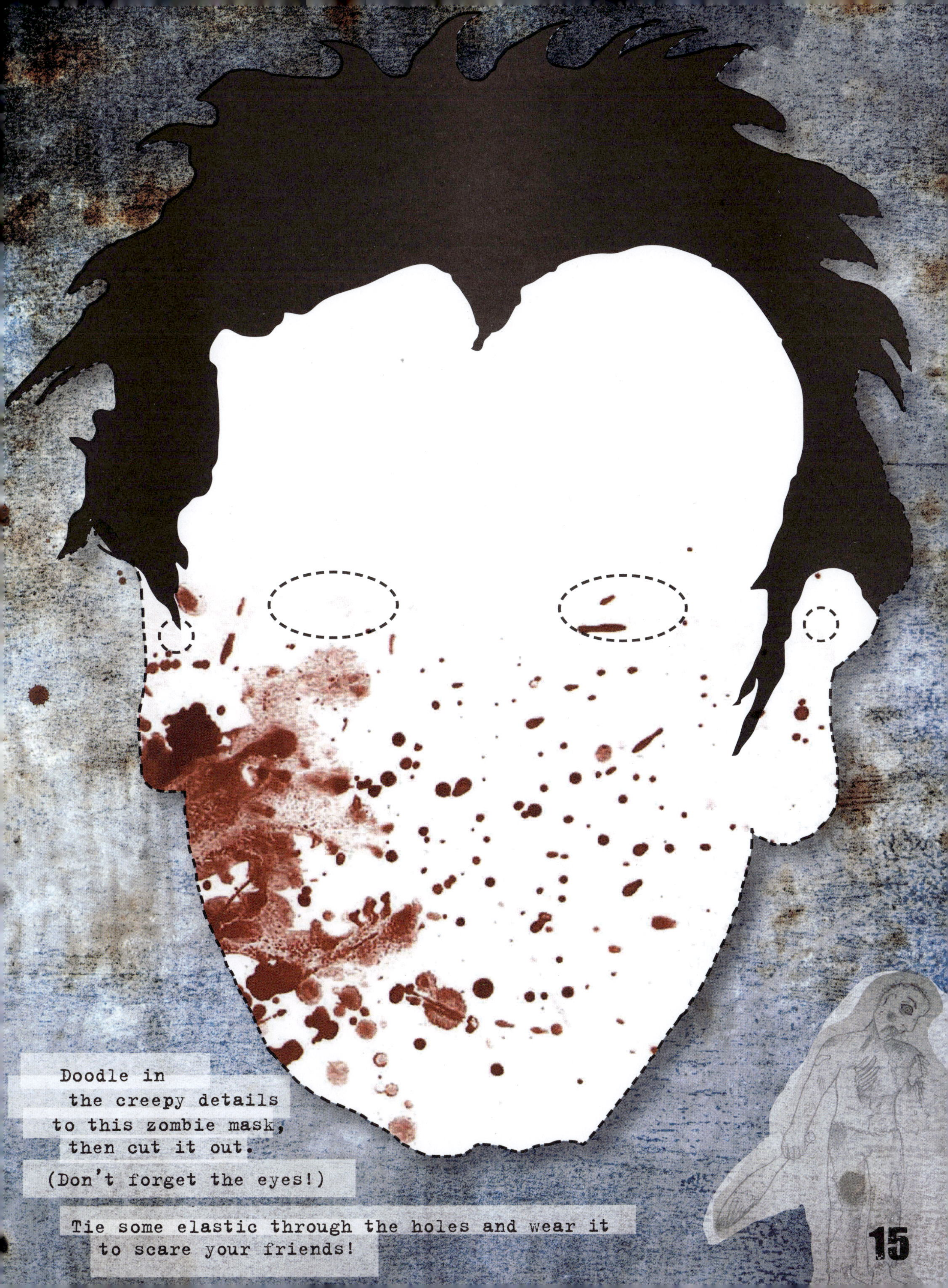
Doodle in
the creepy details
to this zombie mask,
then cut it out.
(Don't forget the eyes!)
Tie some elastic through the holes and wear it
to scare your friends!

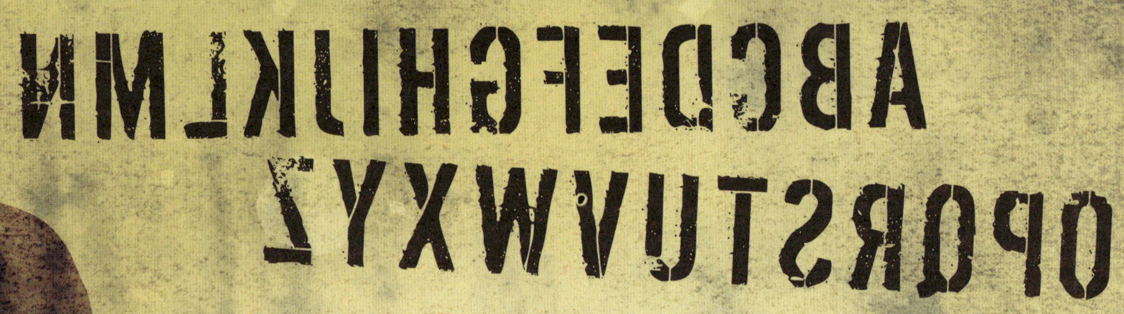

Place your
mirror here
to reveal
the sinister message.

MURDER

Write an evil
message backward and
view it
in the mirror.
Use some creepy fonts
for a scary effect!
Sample above.

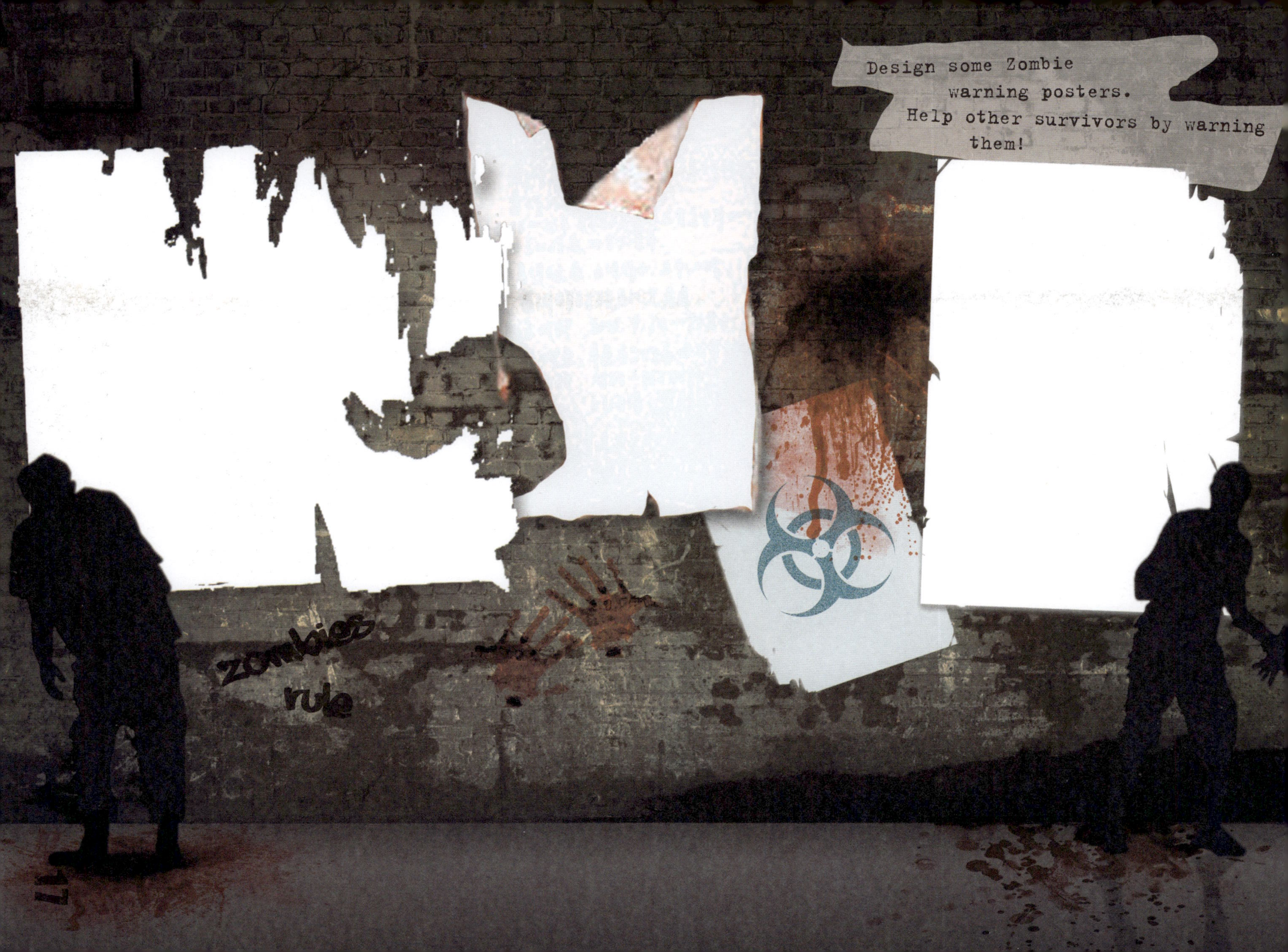
Design some Zombie
warning posters.
Help other survivors by warning
them!
zombies
rule

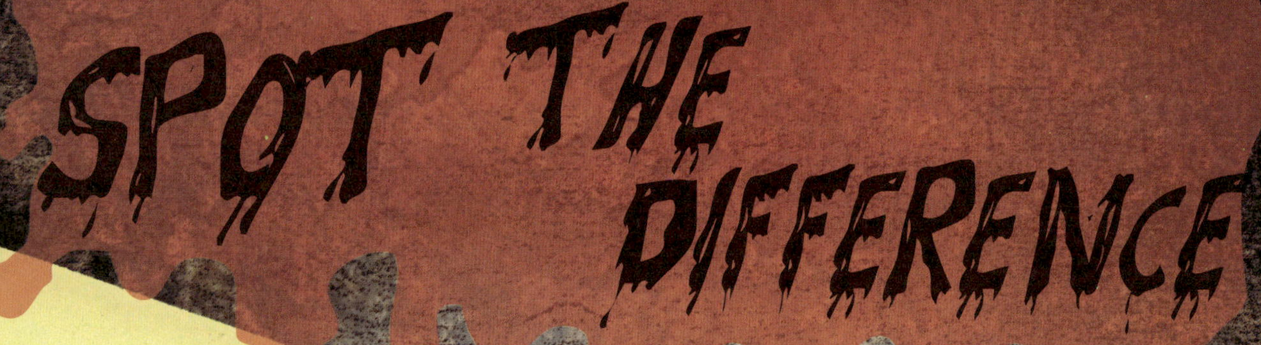

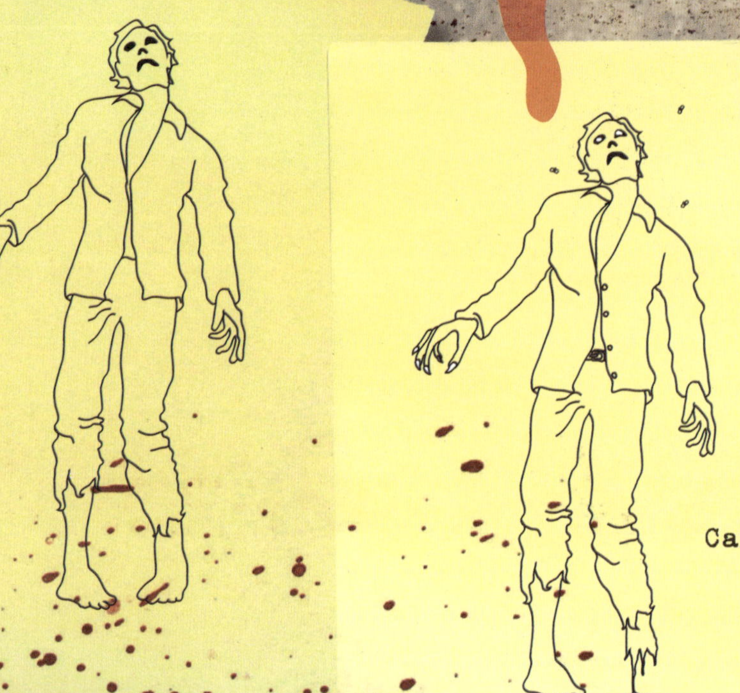

Can you spot the
6 differences
between these
2 zombies?

ZOMBIES OWE A GREAT DEAL OF THEIR POPULARITY TO FILM WRITER DIRECTOR GEORGE A. ROMERO

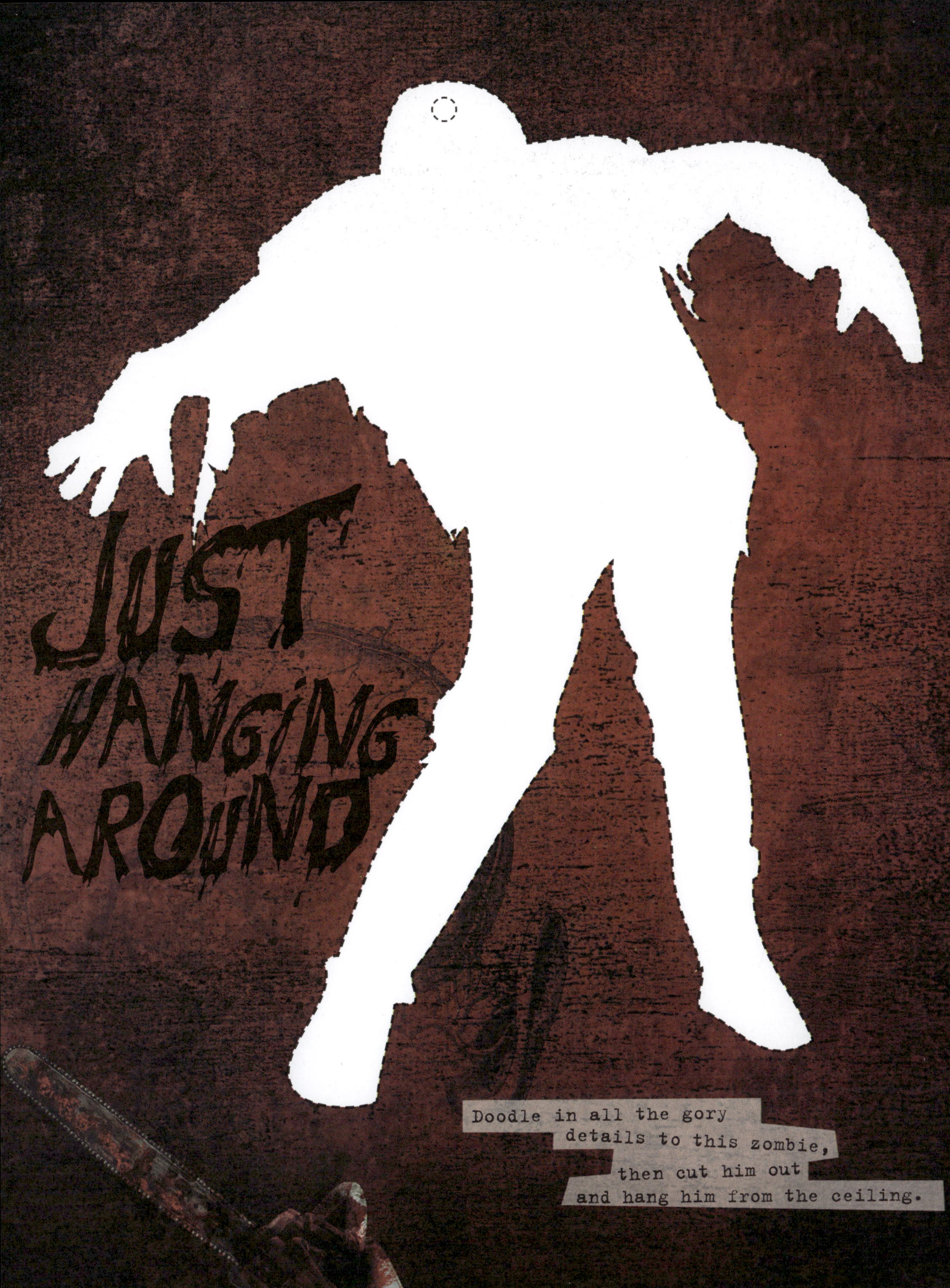
JUST HANGING AROUND
Doodle in all the gory
details to this zombie,
then cut him out
and hang him from the ceiling.

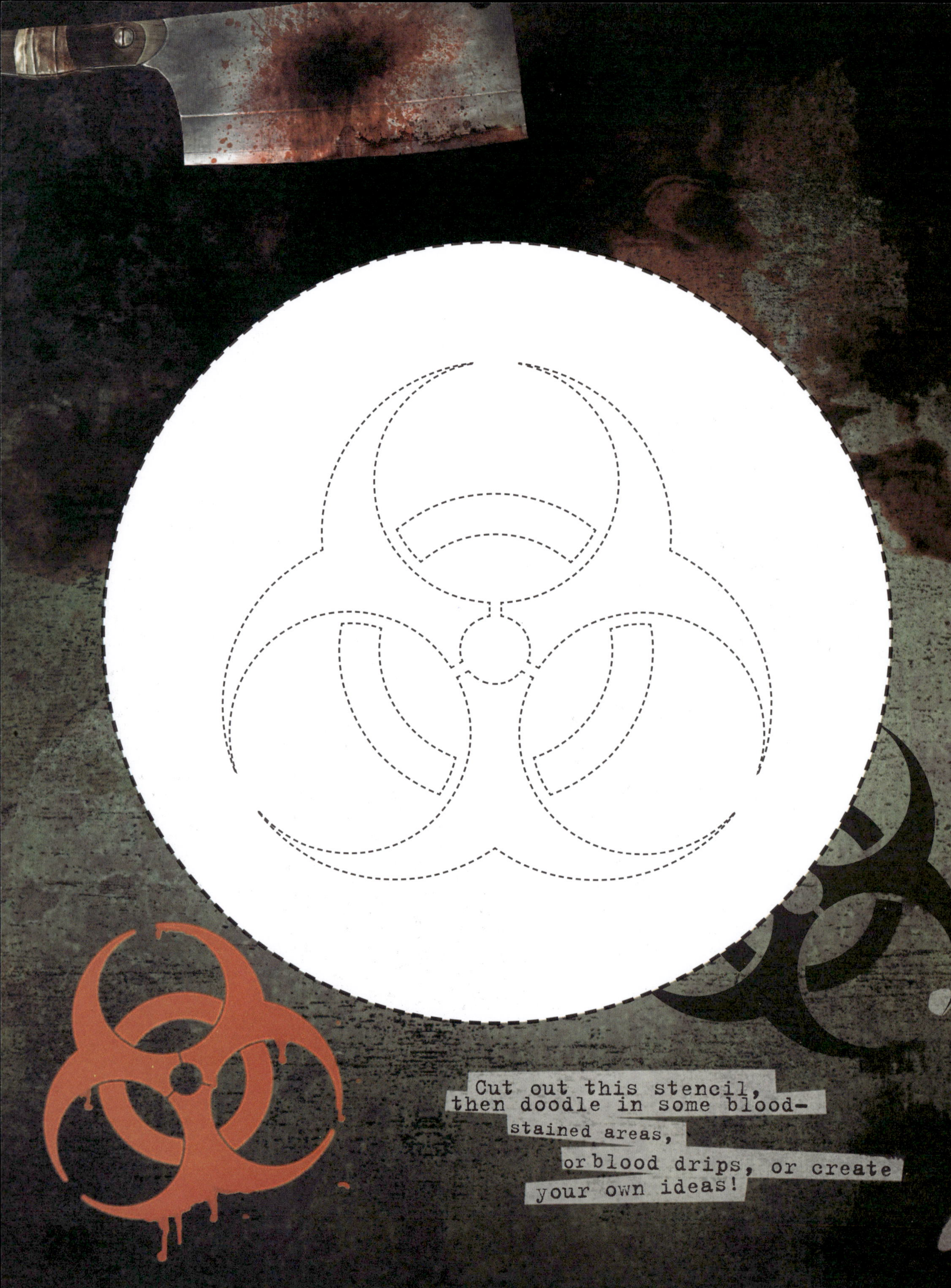
Cut out this stencil,
then doodle in some blood-
stained areas,
or blood drips, or create
your own ideas!

Doodle your zombie T-shirt design.

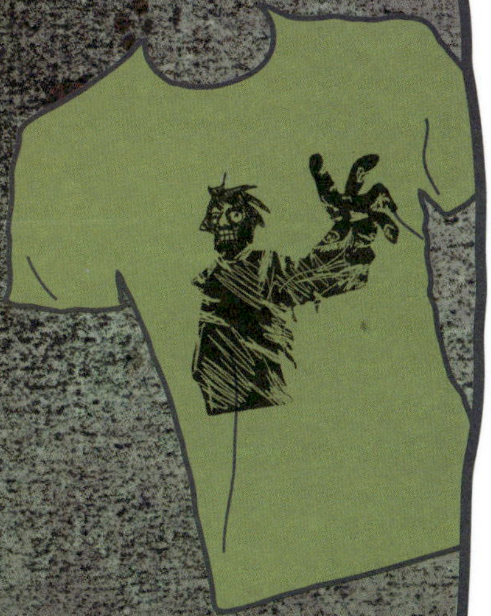

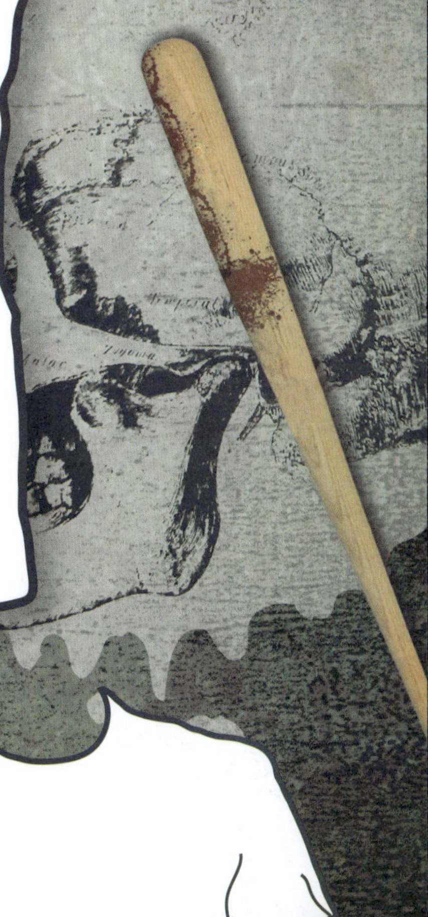

Try some practice designs here first.

BLOODY HELL!

(nonalcholic)

Ingredients

2 ice cubes
1 lemon, juice only
6 dashes Worcestershire sauce
3 dashes Tabasco sauce
5 fl. oz. tomato juice
pinch of salt and freshly ground black pepper

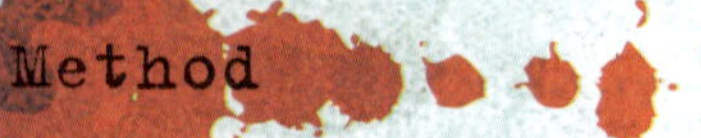

Method

1. Place the ice into a tall glass.
2. Add the lemon juice, Worcestershire sauce, Tabasco sauce, and tomato juice. Stir well.
3. Adjust the seasoning, to taste, with salt and pepper, and serve immediately.

Warning
adult assistance recommended for a safe result!

79 gallons OF fake blood WAS USED IN THE FINAL SCENE OF THE FILM **BRAINDEAD** (1992)

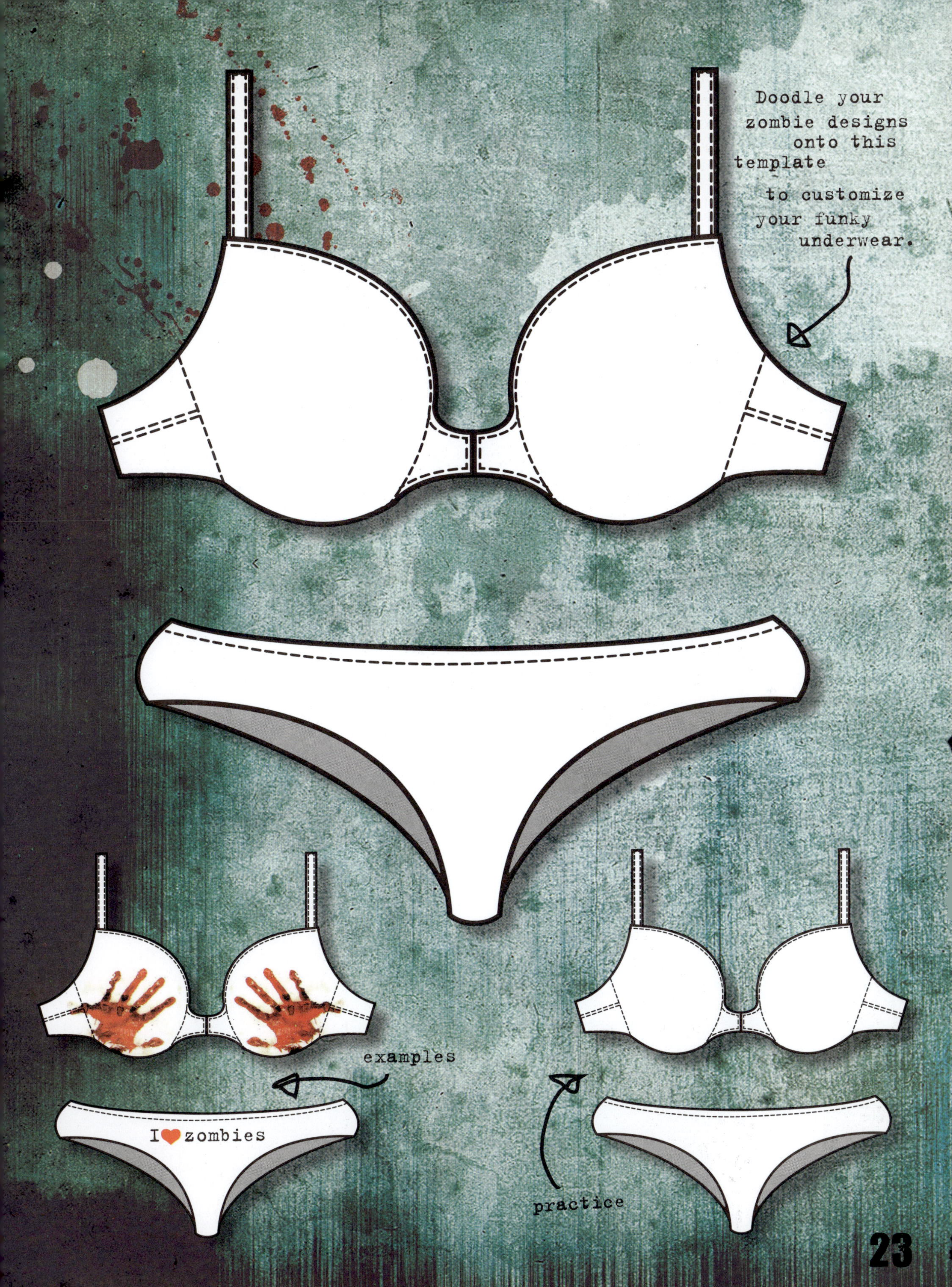
Doodle your zombie designs onto this template to customize your funky underwear.
examples
I ♥ zombies
practice

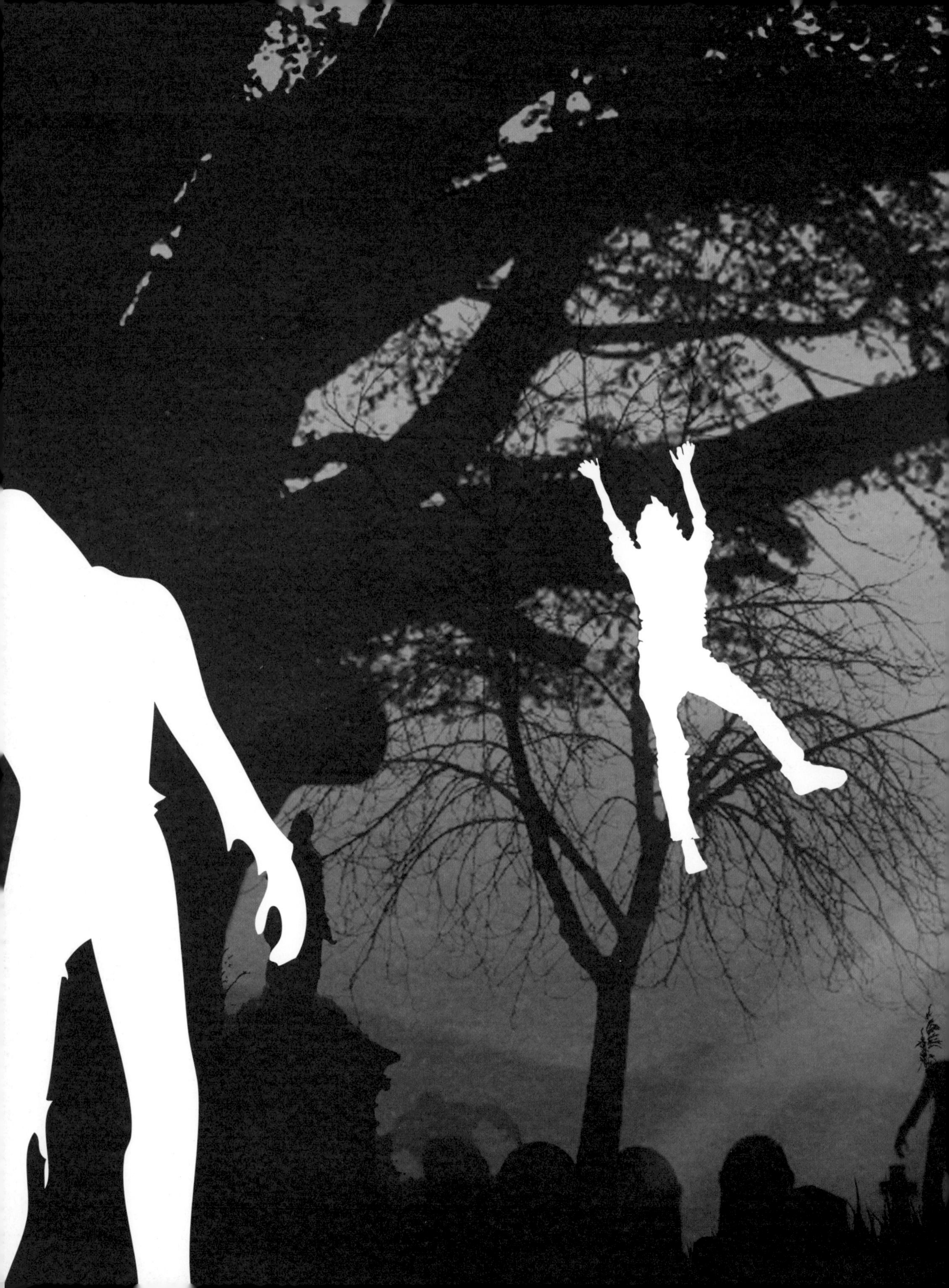

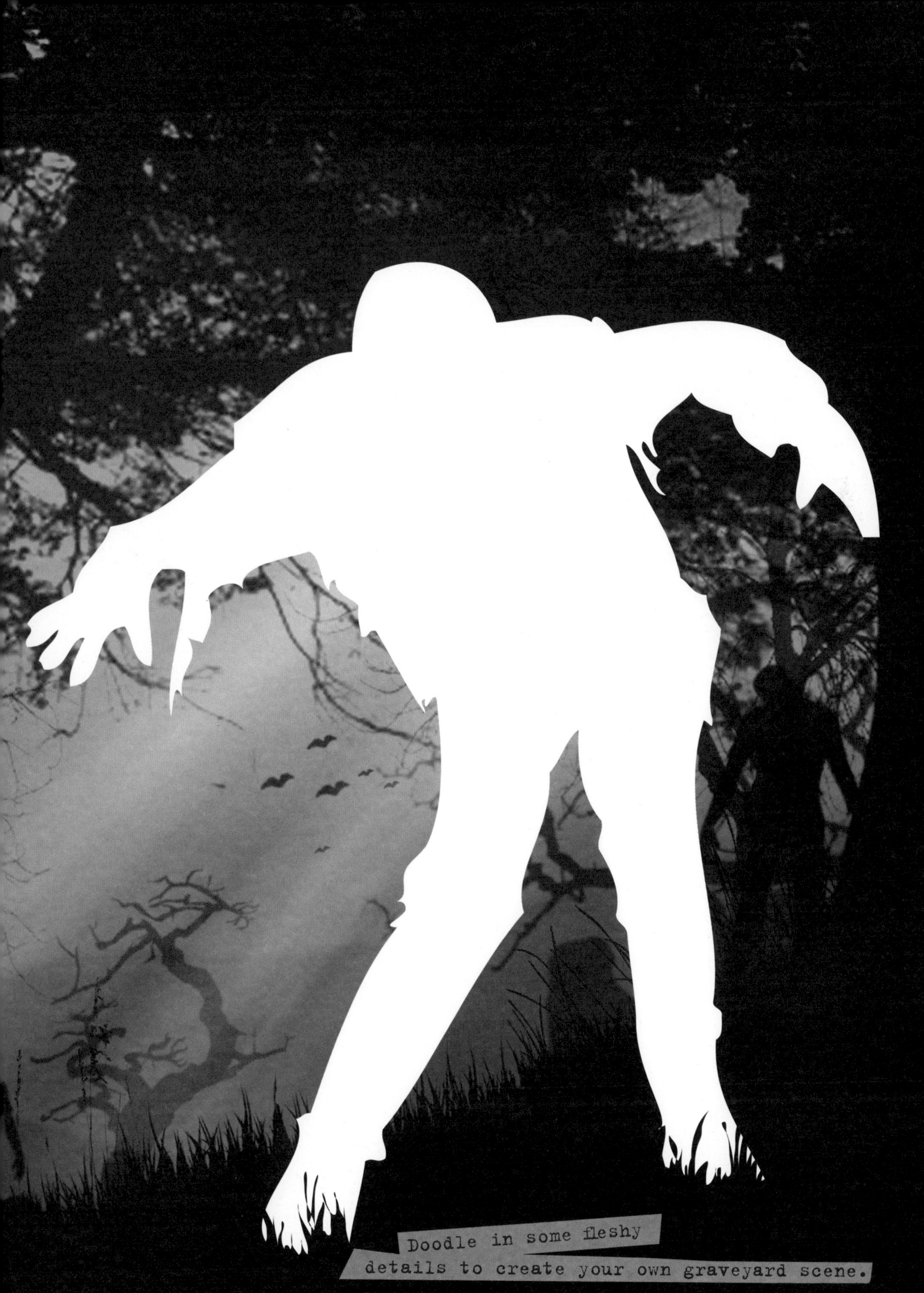

Doodle in some fleshy details to create your own graveyard scene.

Doodle and design name tags for your guests at your awesome spooky party!

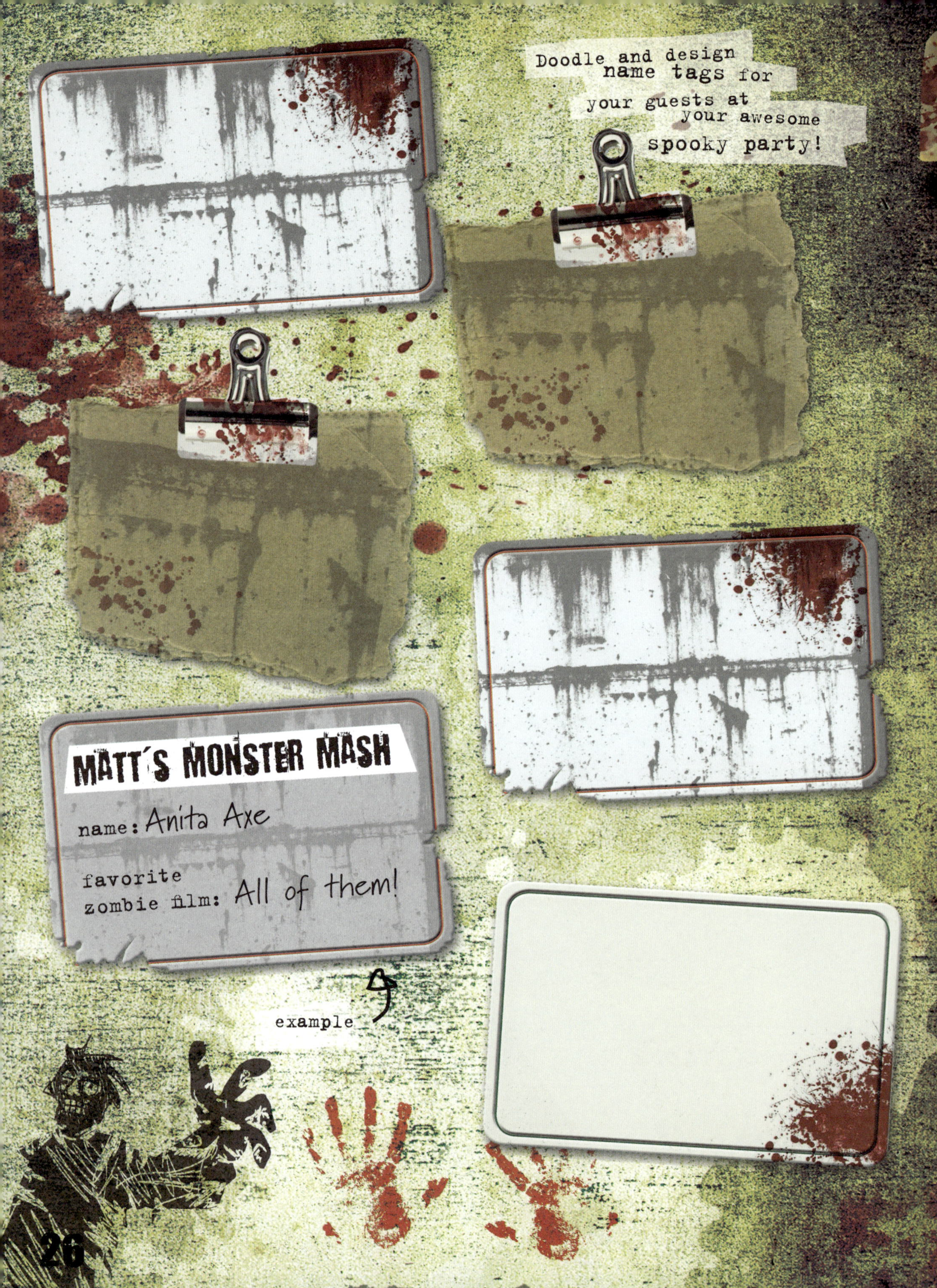

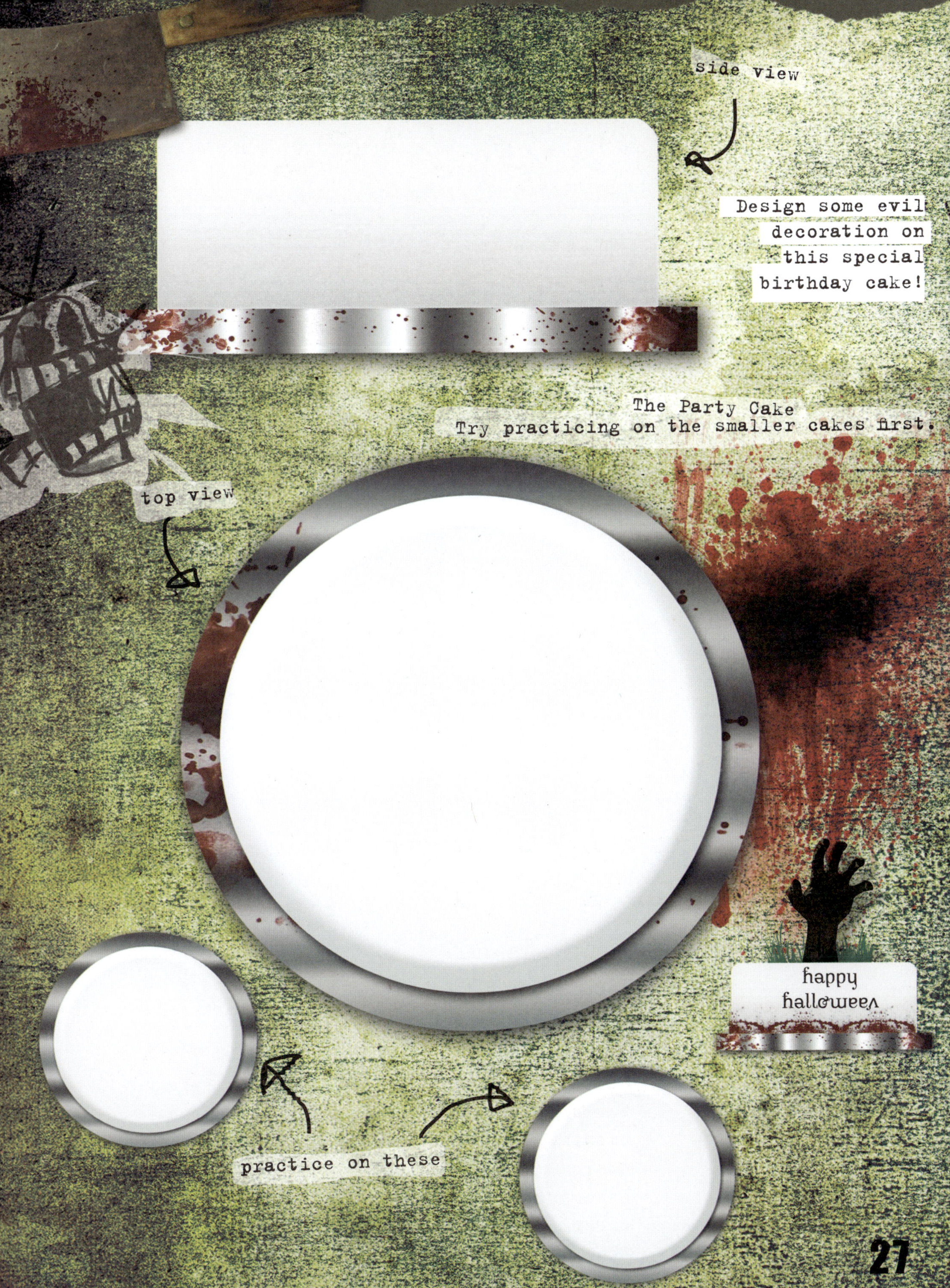
side view
Design some evil decoration on this special birthday cake!
The Party Cake
Try practicing on the smaller cakes first.
top view
happy halloween
practice on these

WORD SEARCH 2

o	e	e	r	d	l	e	k	r	e	r	f	f	c
e	h	r	l	e	r	w	b	s	h	b	y	g	g
t	a	s	v	e	v	y	a	o	a	p	e	r	s
n	e	o	c	l	u	a	r	s	e	m	a	a	p
a	h	r	d	n	a	r	e	e	n	s	s	g	m
s	x	o	d	r	o	b	r	l	t	i	g	a	r
t	e	e	p	r	a	c	i	e	c	e	a	a	g
l	a	m	r	l	u	y	n	n	u	t	m	h	r
d	l	e	l	g	a	c	e	g	n	m	a	e	c
o	t	b	m	u	h	g	r	v	h	a	e	e	c
a	a	e	r	r	o	o	u	l	a	l	c	i	m
t	c	s	a	a	m	f	u	e	l	r	u	o	l
b	g	s	r	b	e	l	l	l	e	s	g	a	e
p	h	a	n	o	g	c	r	w	s	a	e	t	e

- axe
- baseball bat
- cannibal
- chainsaw
- cemetery
- creepy
- foul
- gas mask
- graveyard
- ghoul
- horror
- meat
- meat cleaver
- morgue
- plague
- rags
- shovel
- stench
- terror
- undead

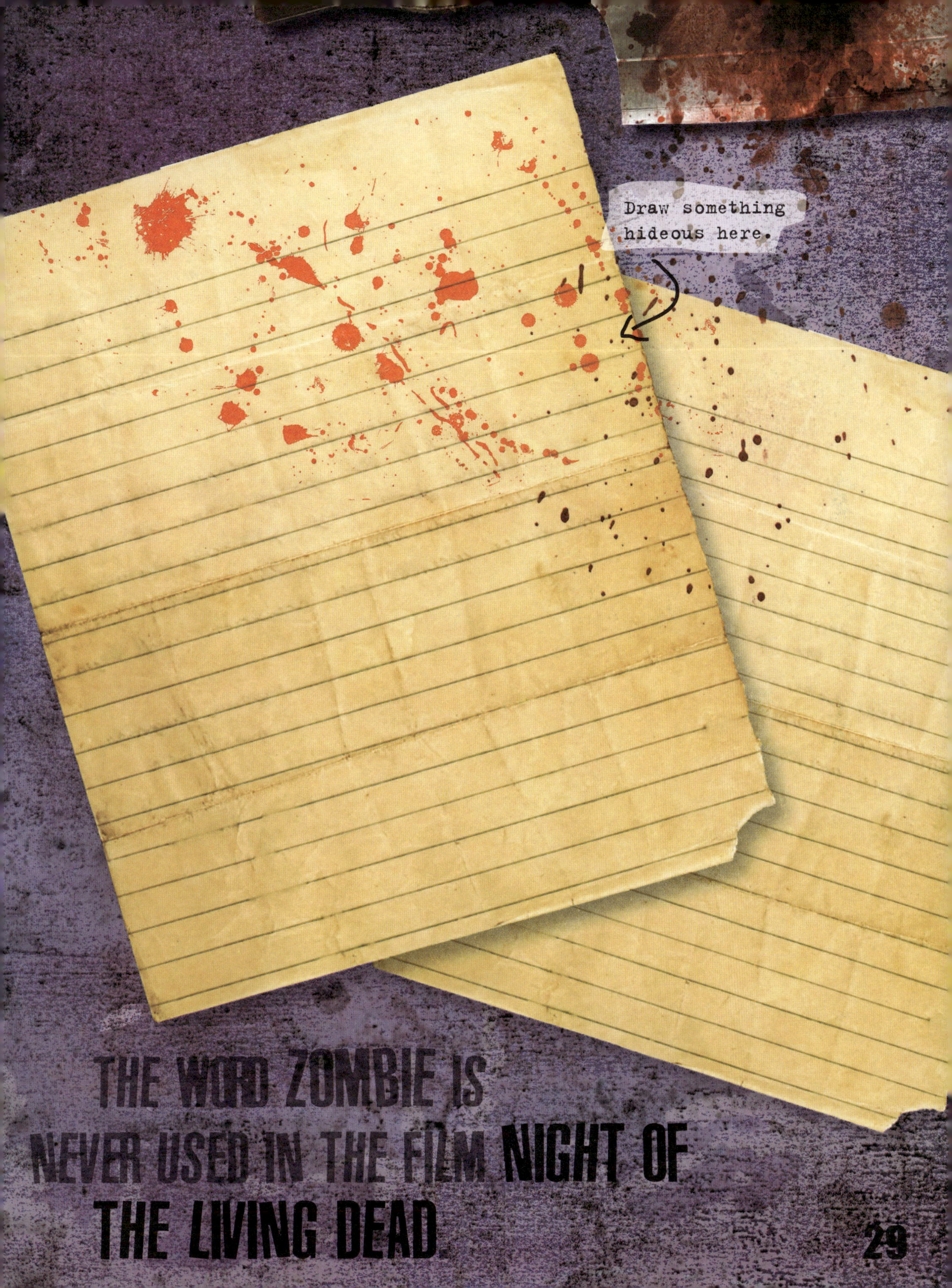

THE WORD ZOMBIE IS NEVER USED IN THE FILM NIGHT OF THE LIVING DEAD.

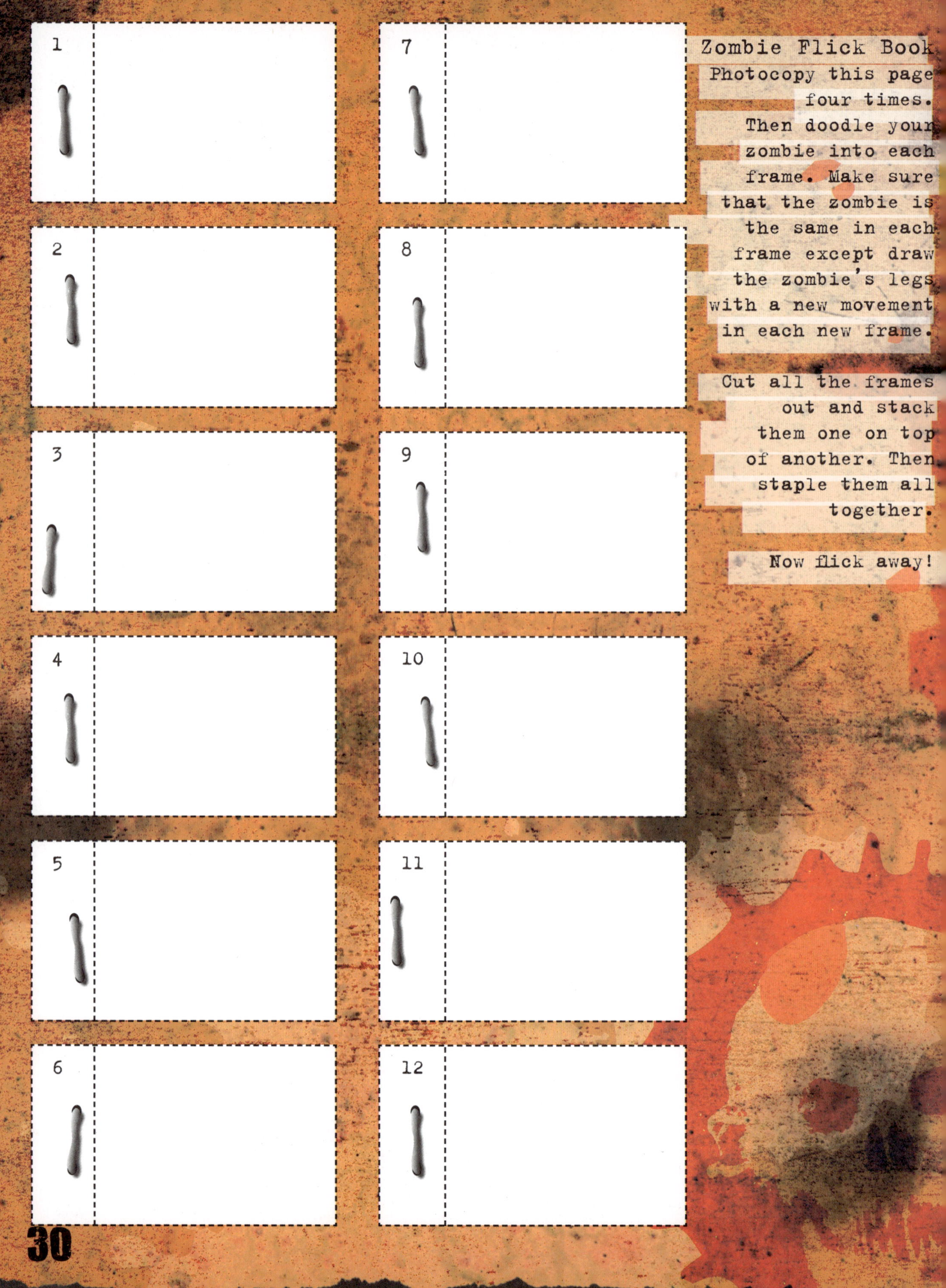

Zombie Flick Book

Photocopy this page four times. Then doodle your zombie into each frame. Make sure that the zombie is the same in each frame except draw the zombie's legs with a new movement in each new frame.

Cut all the frames out and stack them one on top of another. Then staple them all together.

Now flick away!

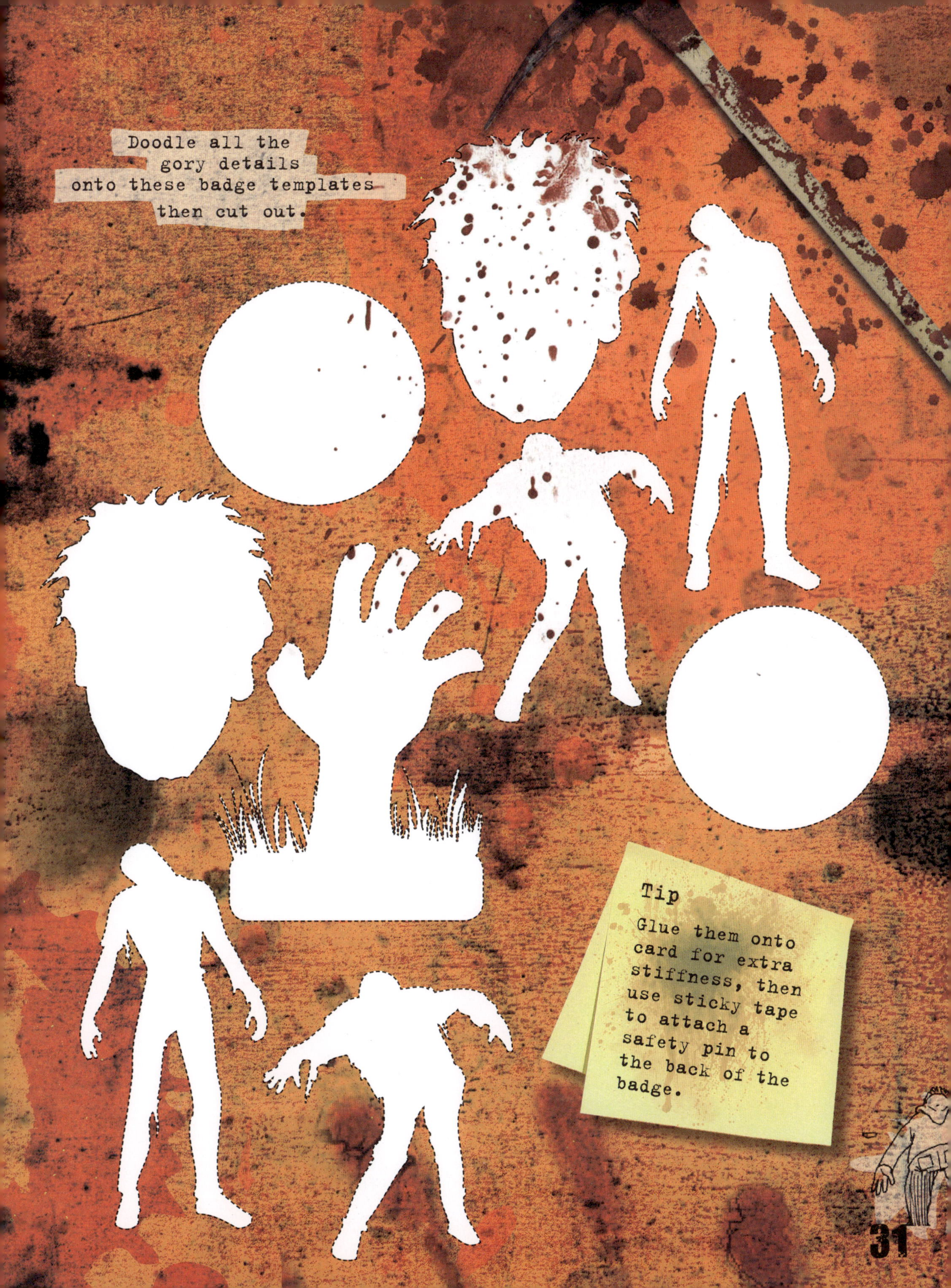
Doodle all the
gory details
onto these badge templates
then cut out.
Tip
Glue them onto
card for extra
stiffness, then
use sticky tape
to attach a
safety pin to
the back of the
badge.

BLOODLINES

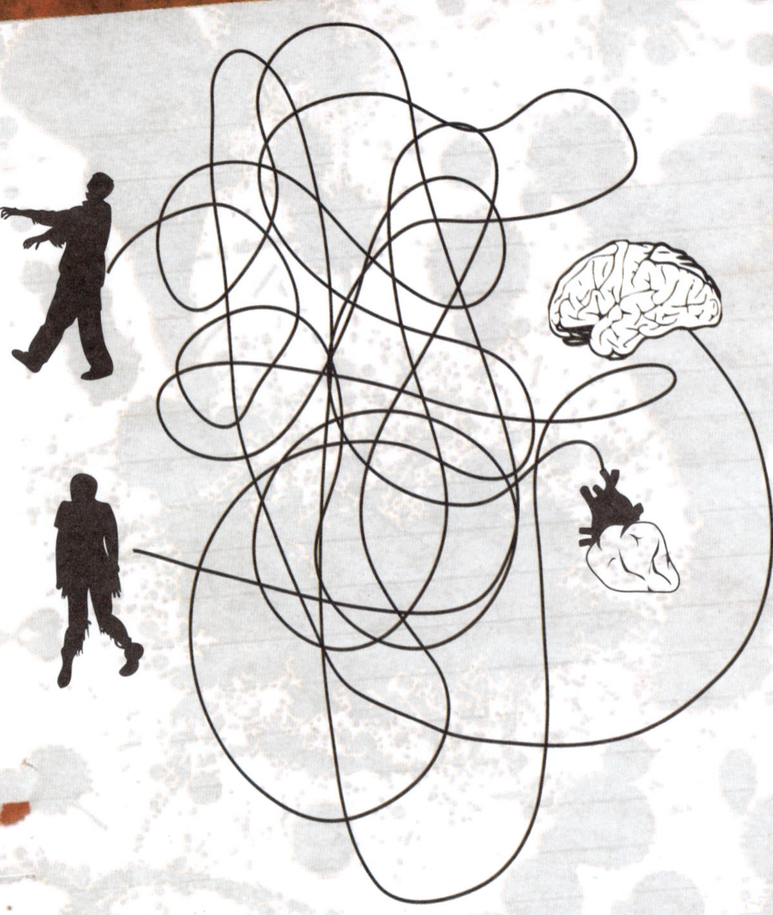

Find out which zombie gets to eat the delicious heart or those juicy brains by following the tangled wiry mess!

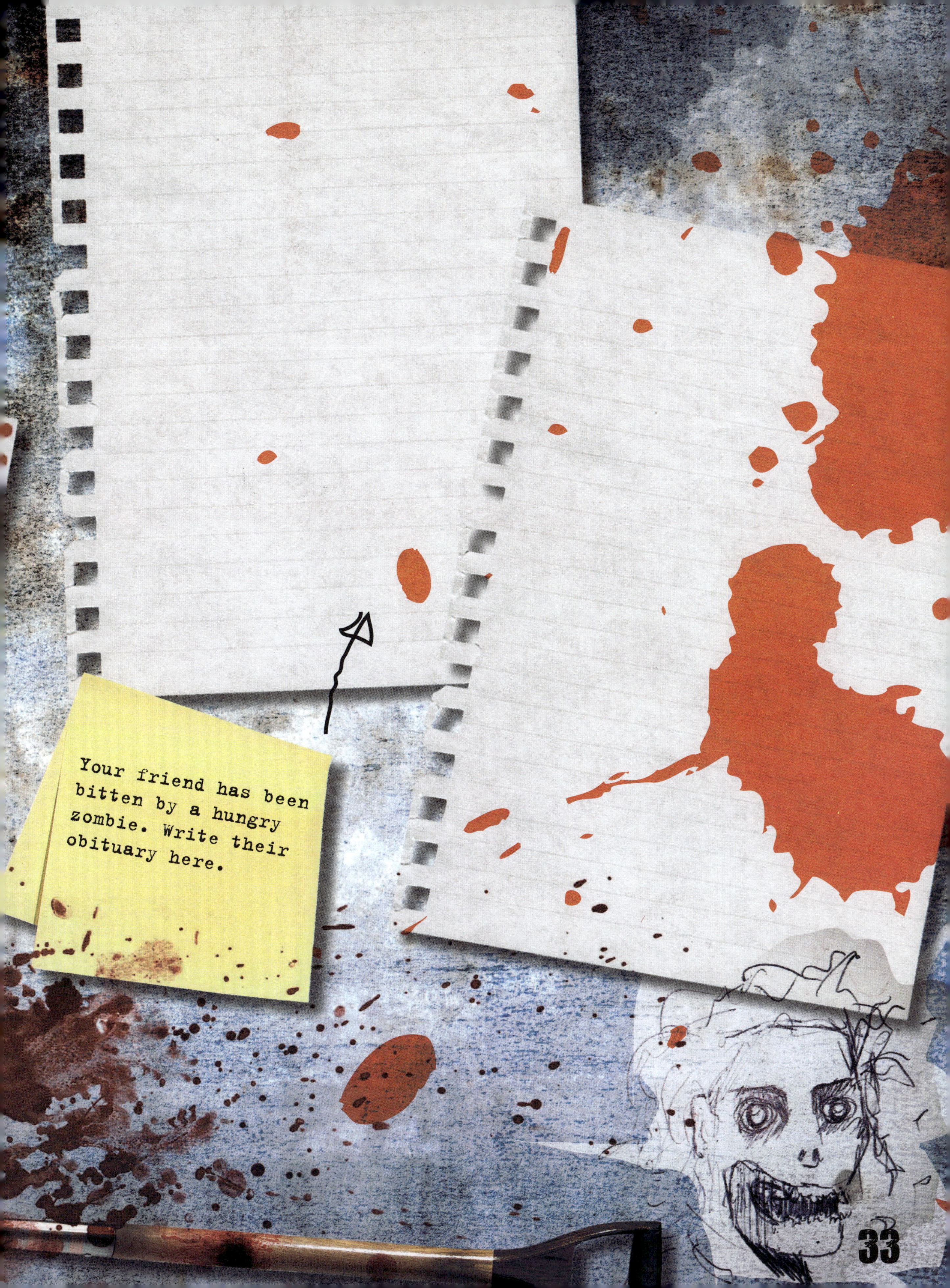
Your friend has been bitten by a hungry zombie. Write their obituary here.

ZOMBIE HANGMAN

Cross off the dead letters.

ABCDEFGHIJKLMNOPQRSTUVWXYZ

Draw your hangman.

Enter your blood-soaked words here.

_ _ _

ABCDEFG HIJKLM NOPQRST UVWXYZ

Cross off the dead letters.

_ _ _

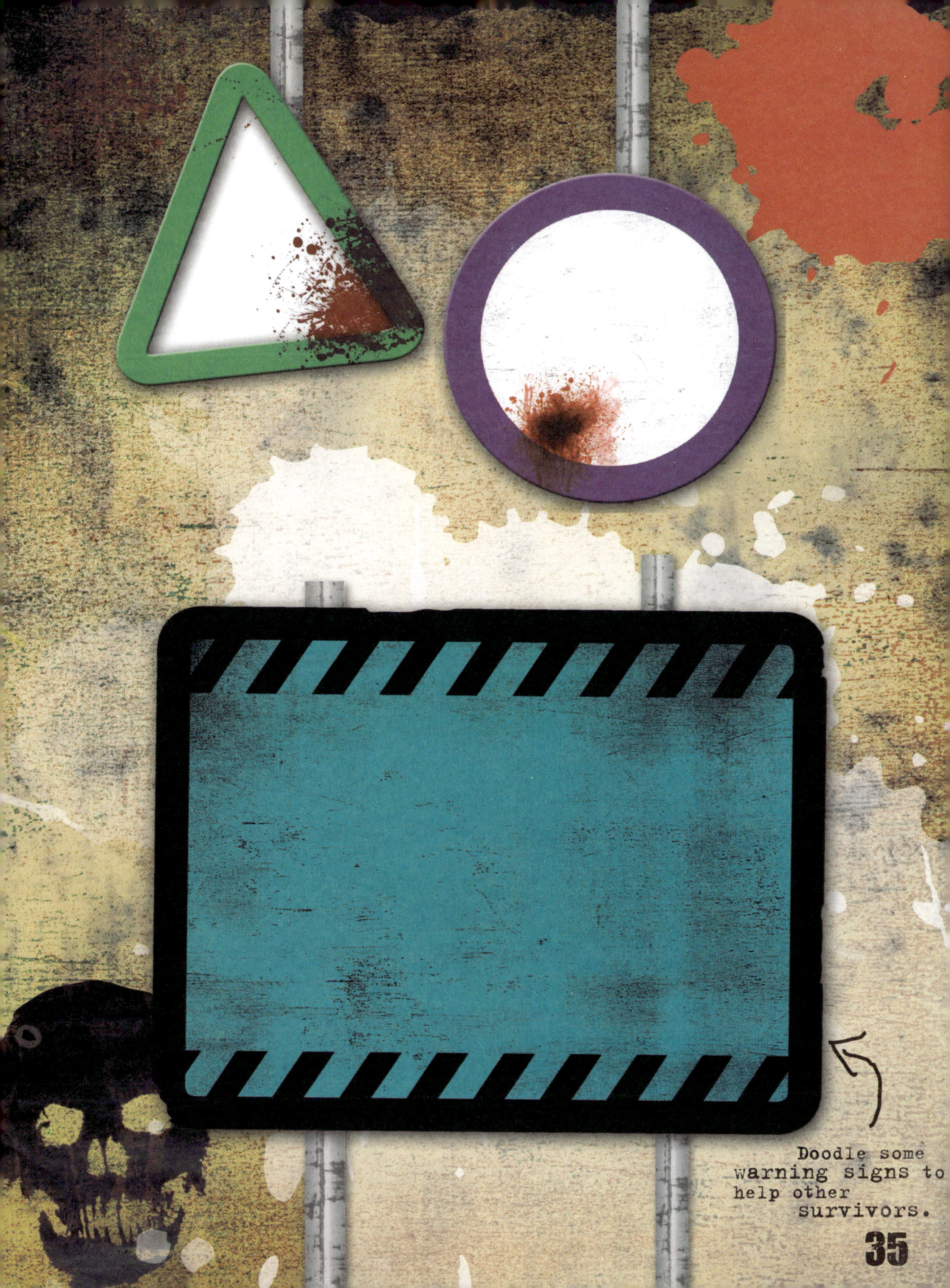

Doodle some warning signs to help other survivors.

SPOT THE DIFFERENCE

The virus is spreading; quick get your mask!
Can you spot the 5 differences between these
2 protective gas masks!

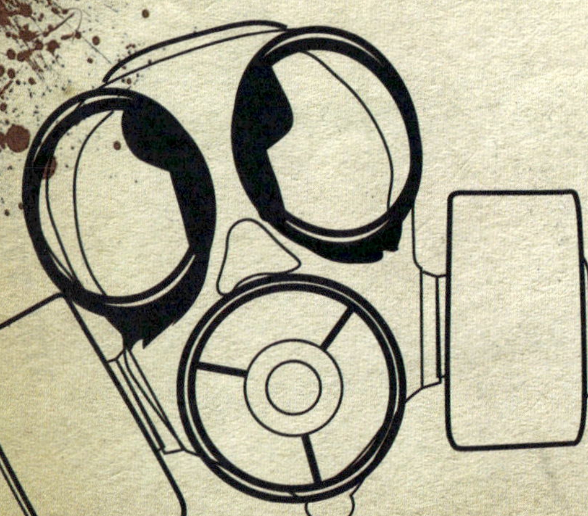

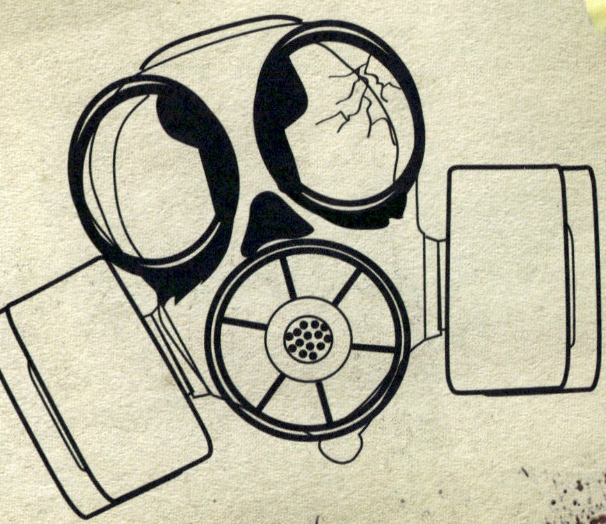

THE COST FOR SHOOTING THE BROOKLYN BRIDGE SCENE IN THE FILM **I AM LEGEND** IS AN ESTIMATED **$5,000,000!**

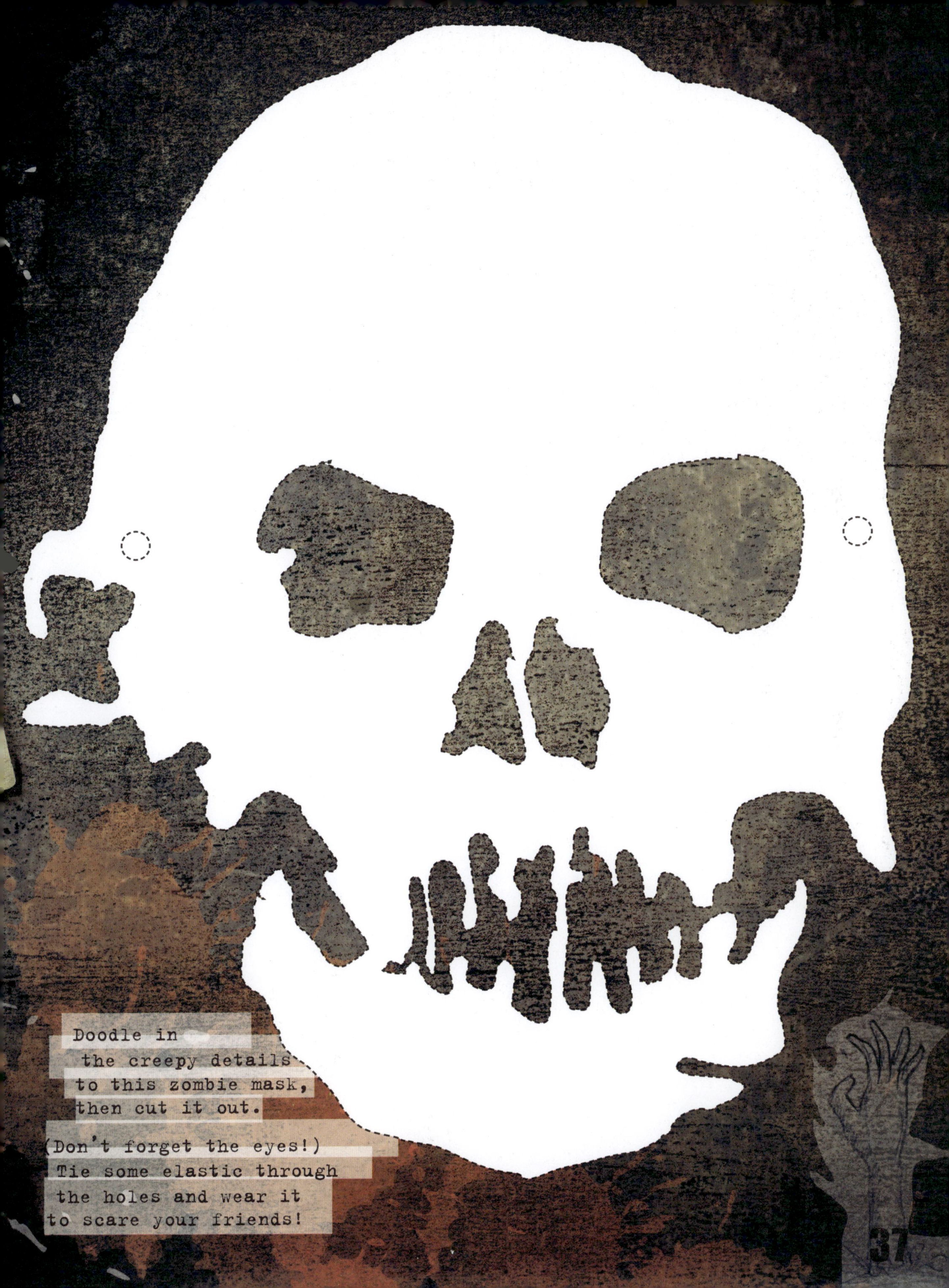

Doodle in
the creepy details
to this zombie mask,
then cut it out.

(Don't forget the eyes!)
Tie some elastic through
the holes and wear it
to scare your friends!

Place your mirror here to reveal the sinister message.

ZOMBIE

Write an evil message backward and view it in the mirror. Use some creepy fonts for a scary effect!

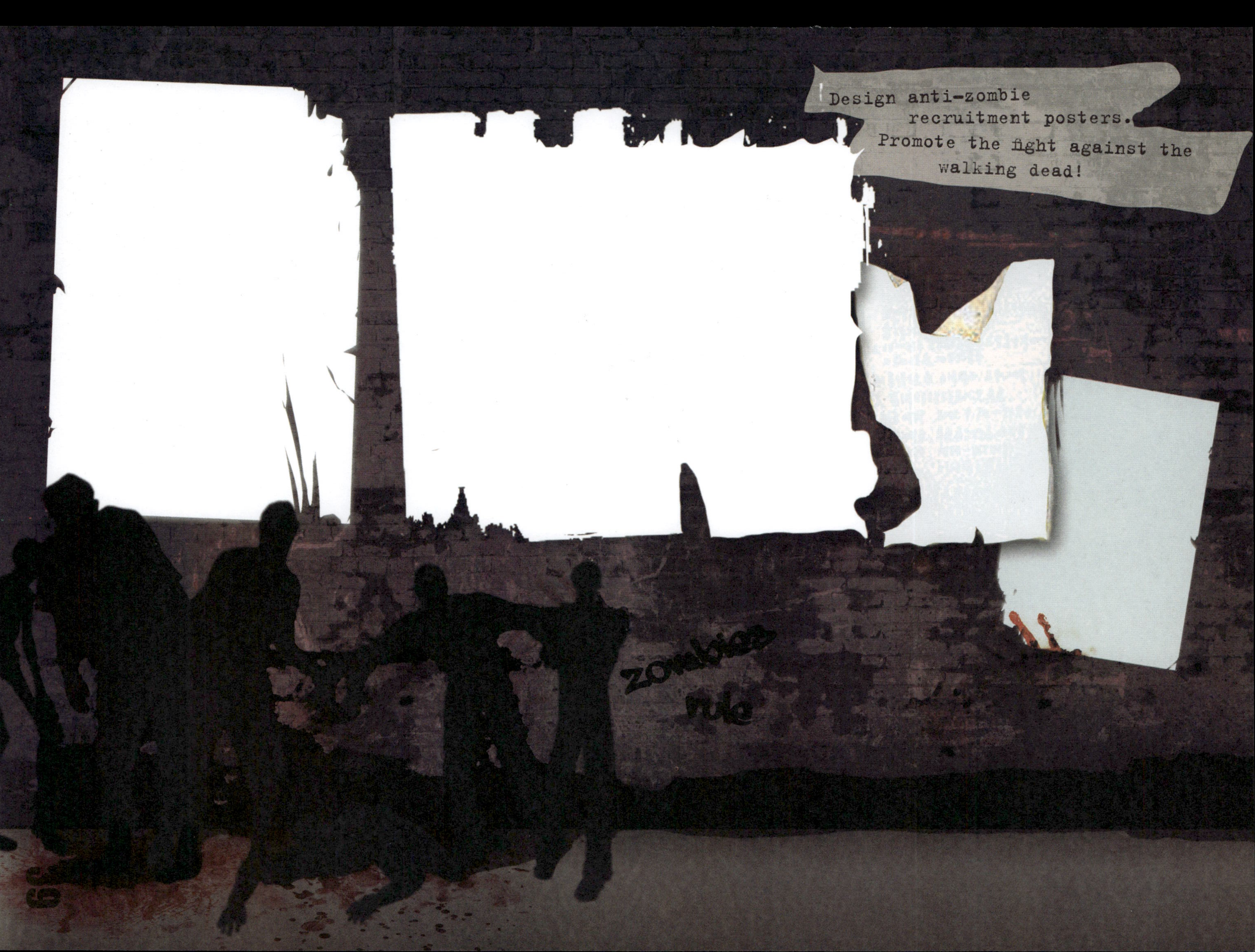
Design anti-zombie
recruitment posters.
Promote the fight against the
walking dead!
zombies
rule

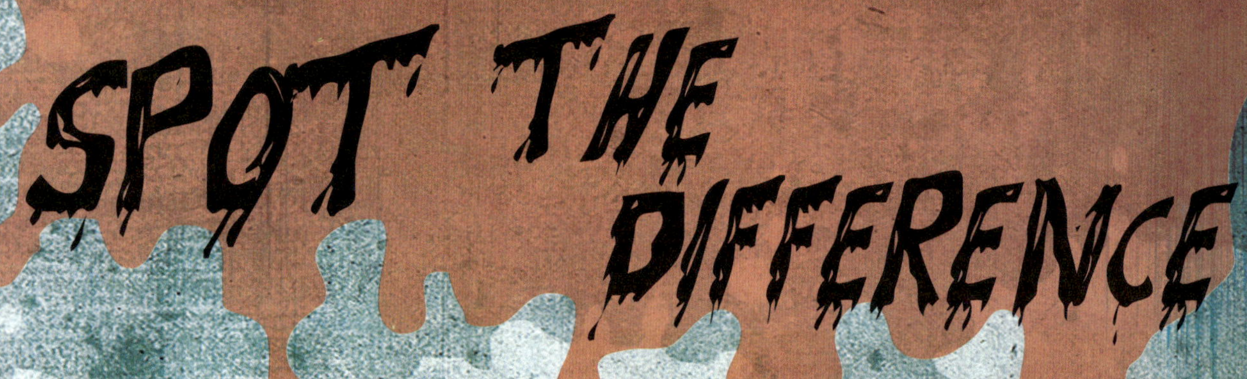

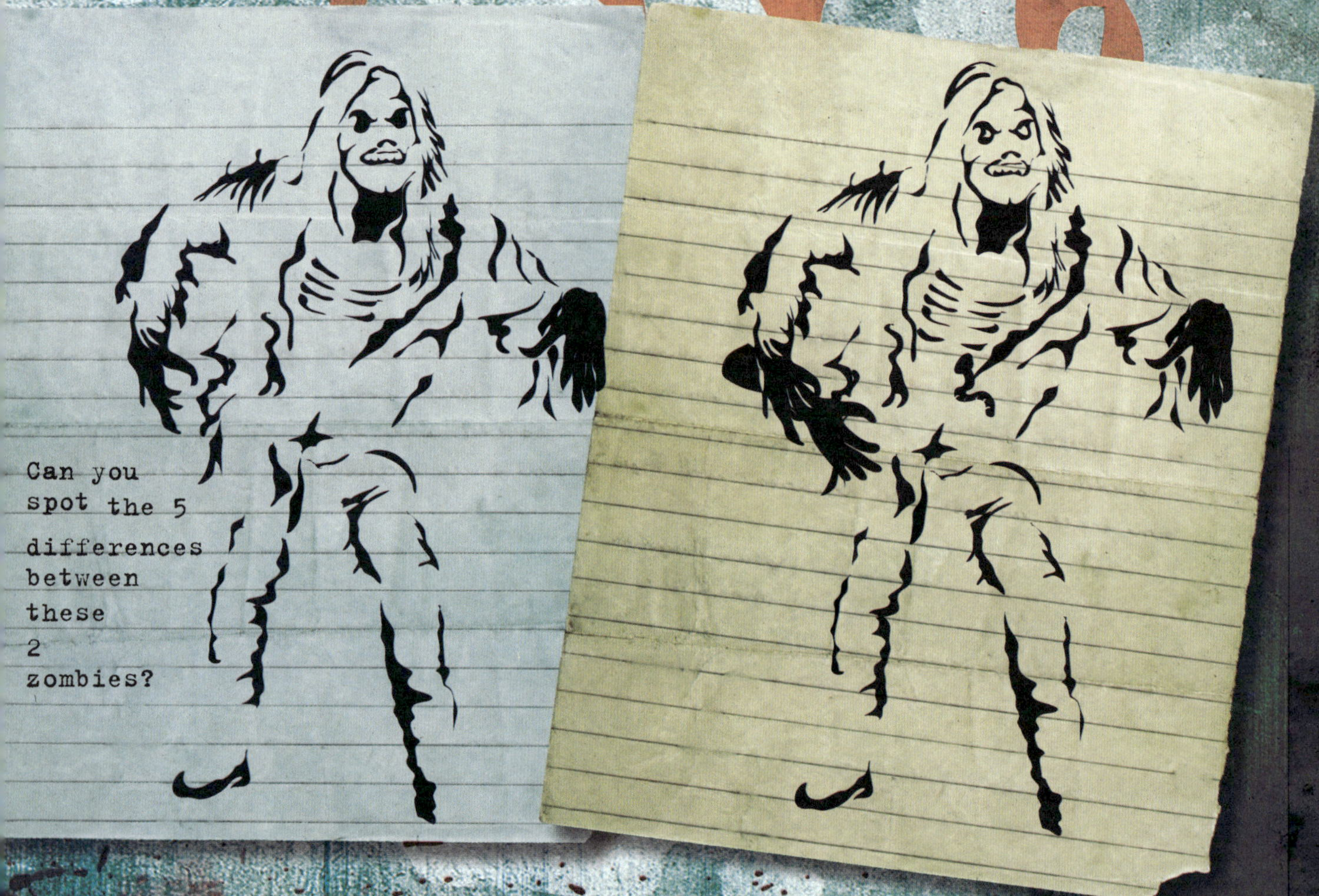

Can you spot the 5 differences between these 2 zombies?

IN THE FILM NIGHT OF THE LIVING DEAD, THE GOODIES (i.e. entrails, meat, etc.) WERE SUPPLIED BY A BUTCHER WHO WAS AN INVESTOR IN THE FILM.

HANGING MOBILE

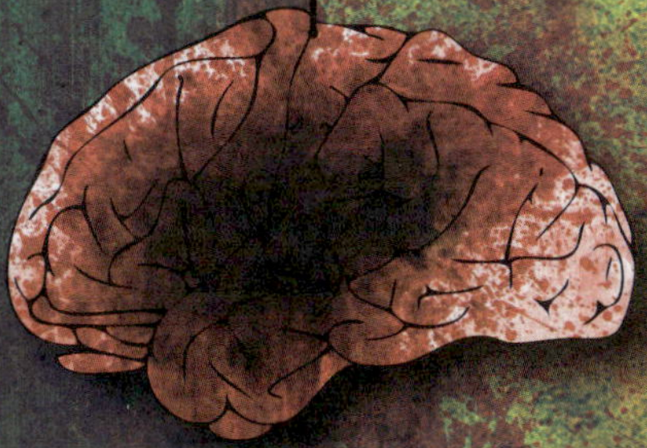

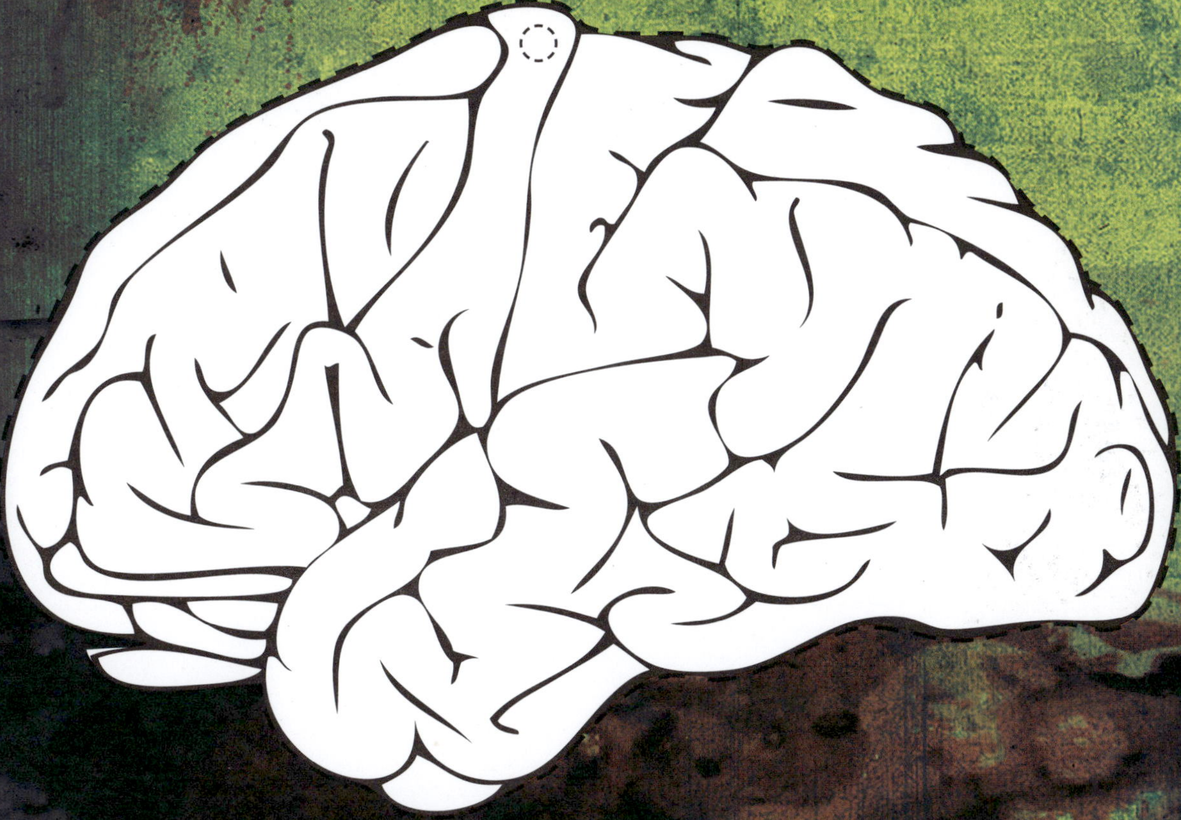

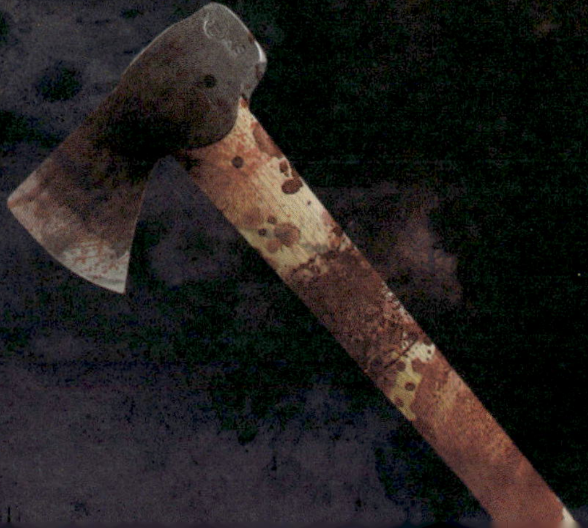

Doodle and design all the gory
details to this brain,
then cut it out
and hang it from the ceiling.

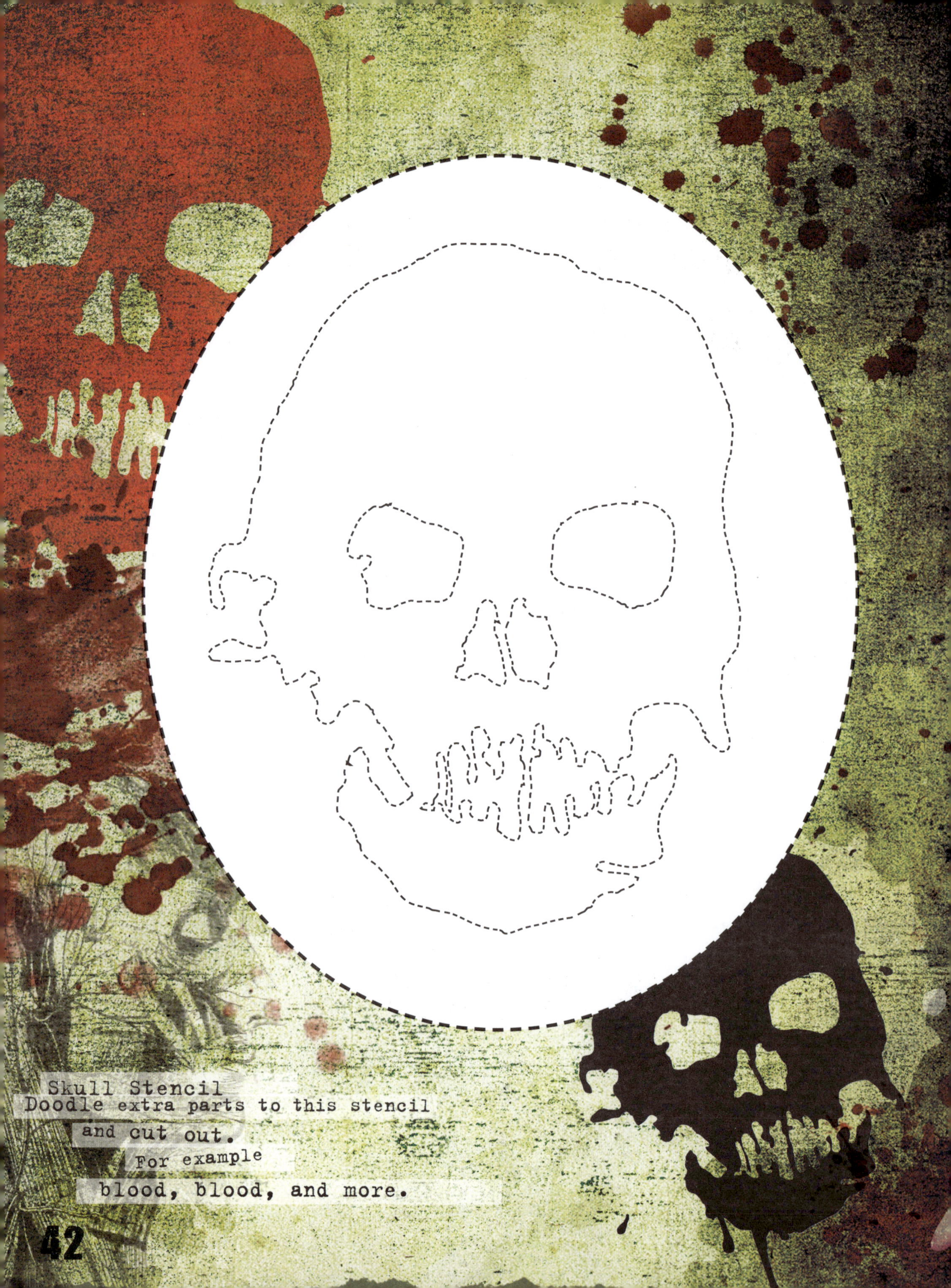

Skull Stencil
Doodle extra parts to this stencil
and cut out.
For example
blood, blood, and more.

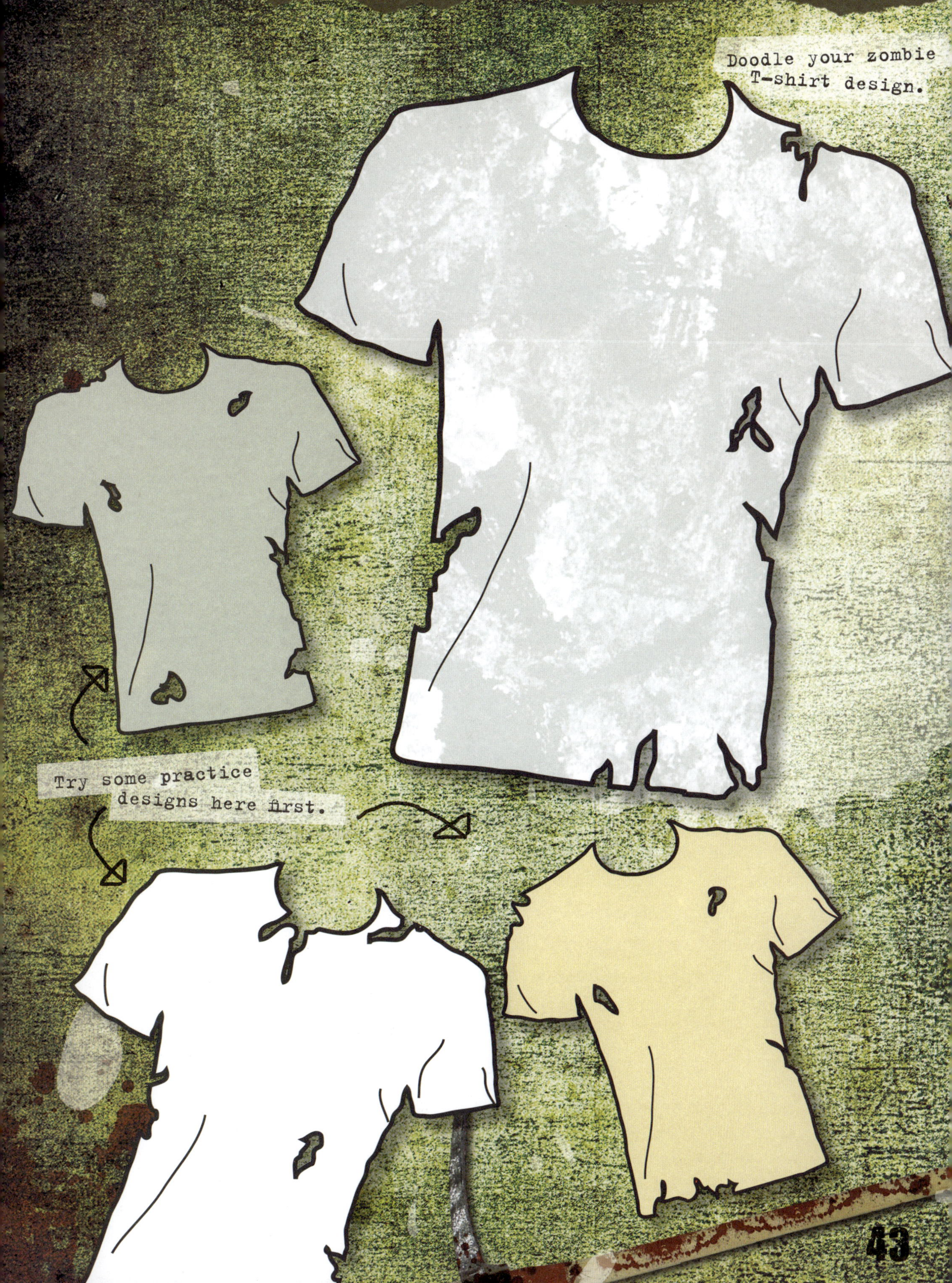
Doodle your zombie
T-shirt design.
Try some practice
designs here first.

DEADMAN'S SOUL

(nonalcholic)

Ingredients

1 oz. lime juice
1 tsp. pineapple juice
1 tsp. papaya juice
1 tsp. superfine sugar

Method

Stir together all the ingredients and pour into a 14-ounce glass three-quarters full of crushed ice. Garnish with mint (either straight or dipped in lime juice and then superfine sugar) and/or fruit. (A particularly nice touch: On a toothpick, impale a lemon slice or pineapple cube between 2 maraschino cherries, and lay this fruit kabob atop of the drink). Supply a straw.

Warning
adult assistance recommended for a safe result!

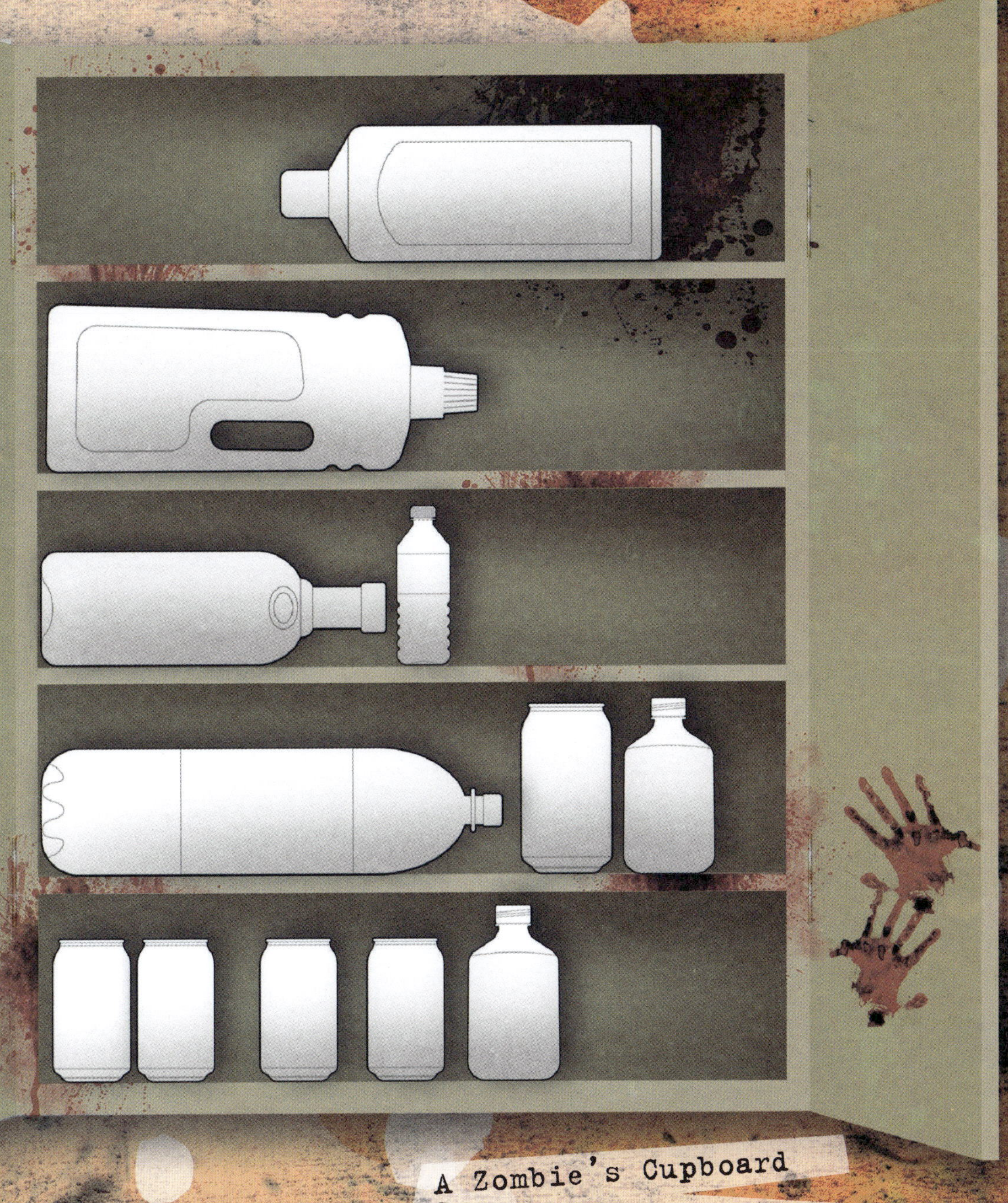

A Zombie's Cupboard

Doodle in some of the gory food that a zombie would keep. For example brains, blood, hands, guts, and eyeballs!

"WHEN THERE'S NO MORE ROOM IN HELL THE DEAD WILL WALK THE EARTH"

DAWN OF THE DEAD

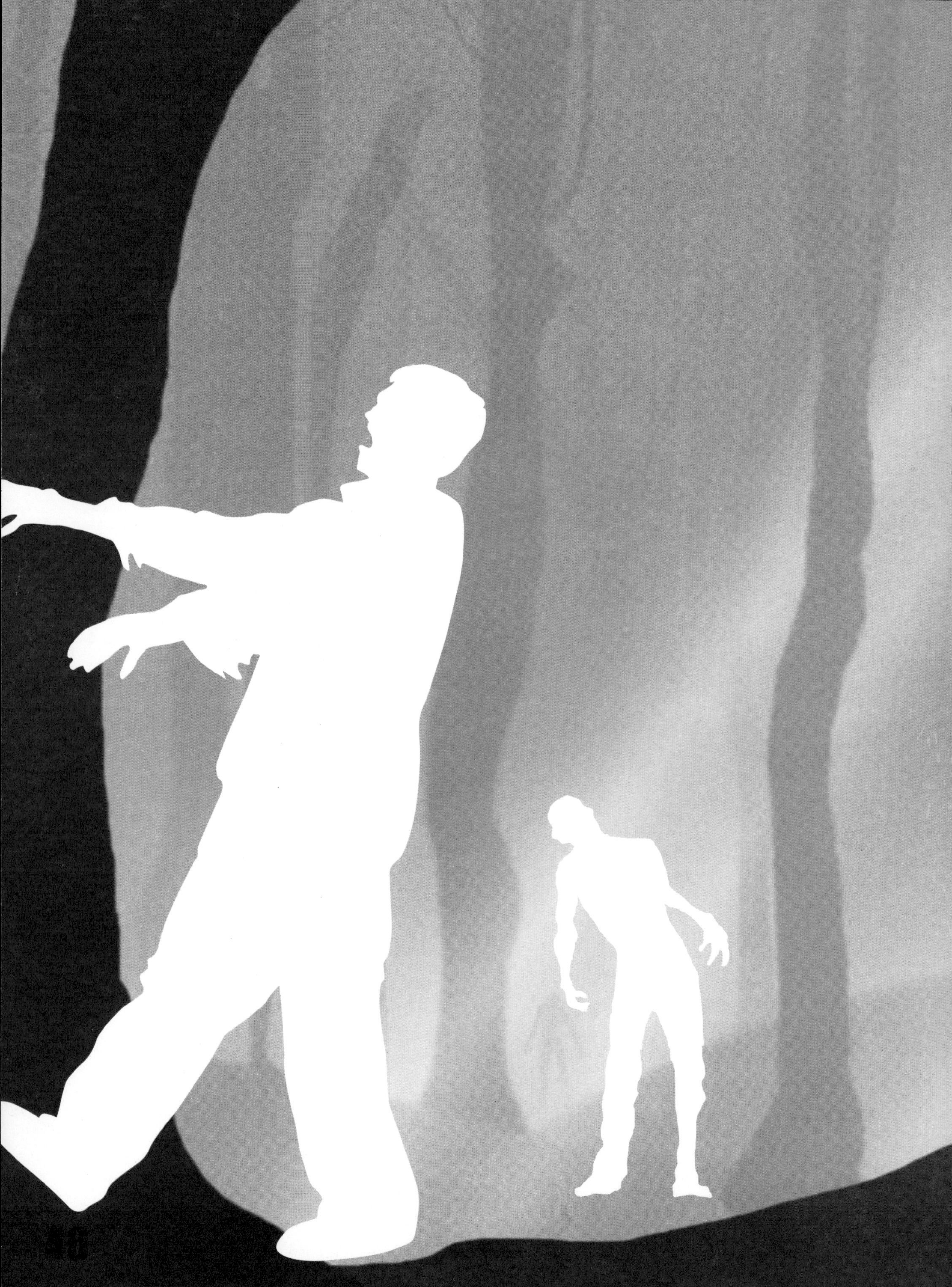

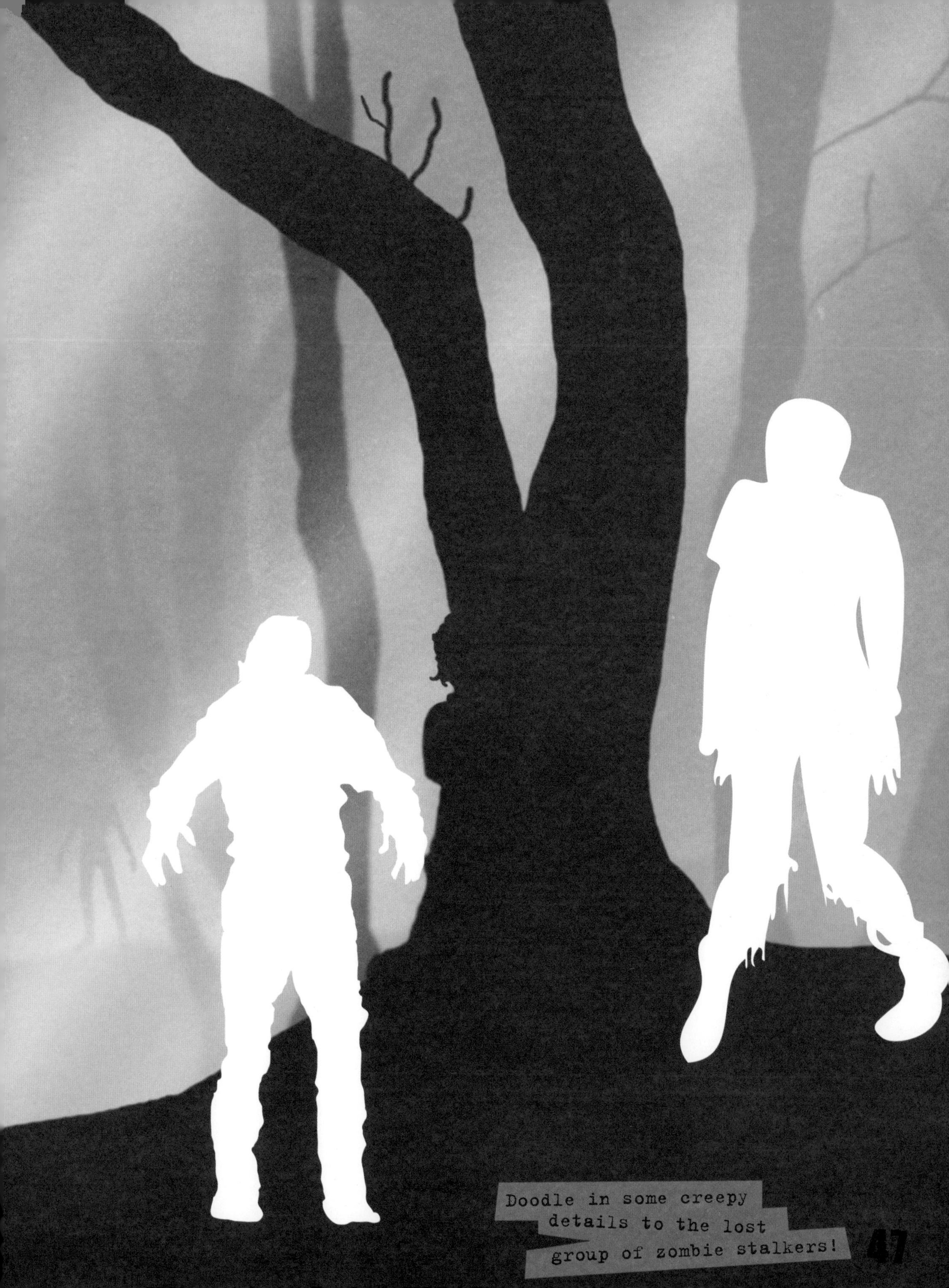
Doodle in some creepy
details to the lost
group of zombie stalkers!

Create tattoo hell!

Doodle and design your gruesome zombie tattoo; it can be a tattoo to warn others, or a logo for your zombie slayer group!

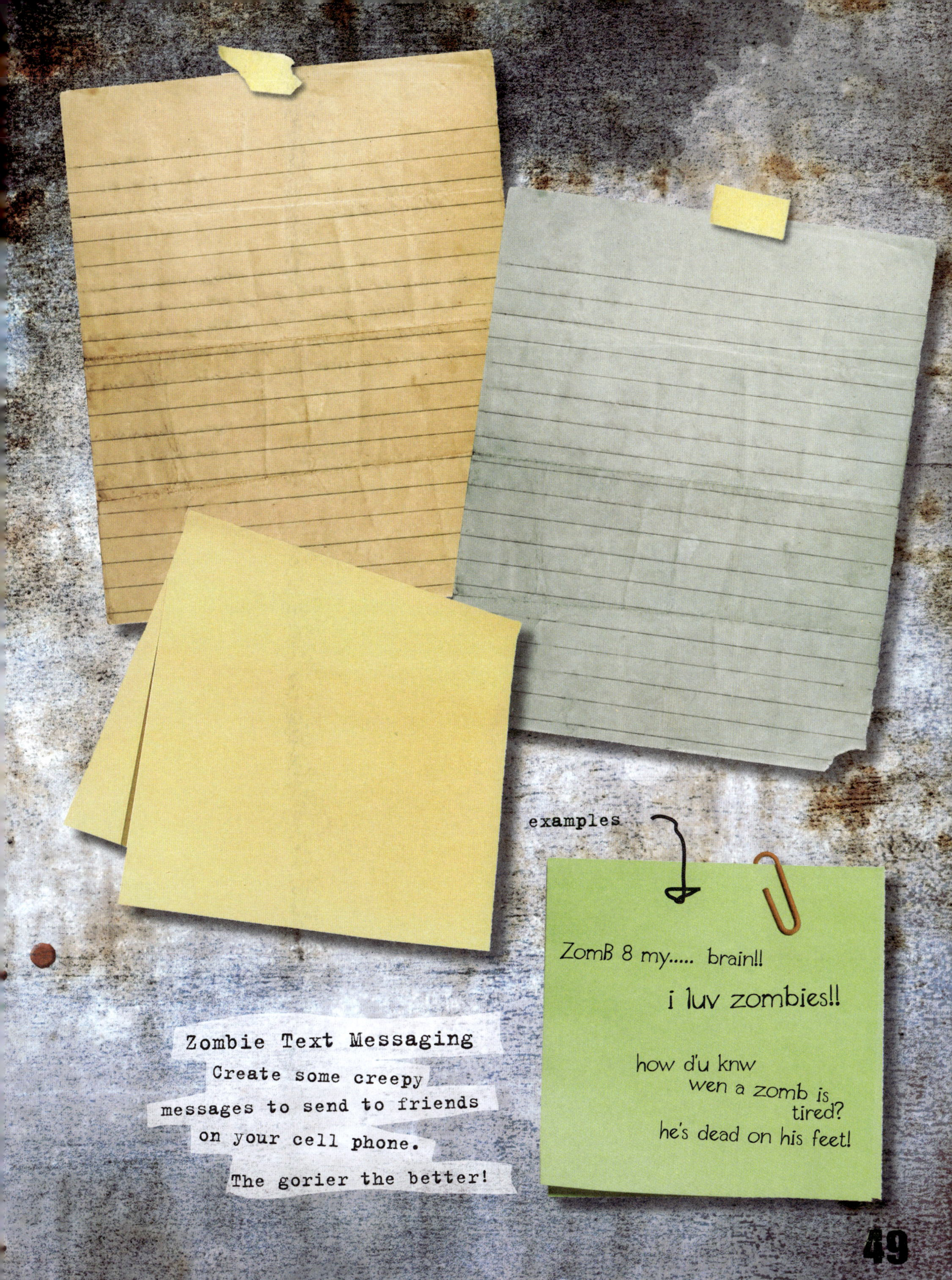

Zombie Text Messaging

Create some creepy messages to send to friends on your cell phone.

The gorier the better!

ZOMBIE SURVIVAL KIT

weapons	first aid	necessities

necessities

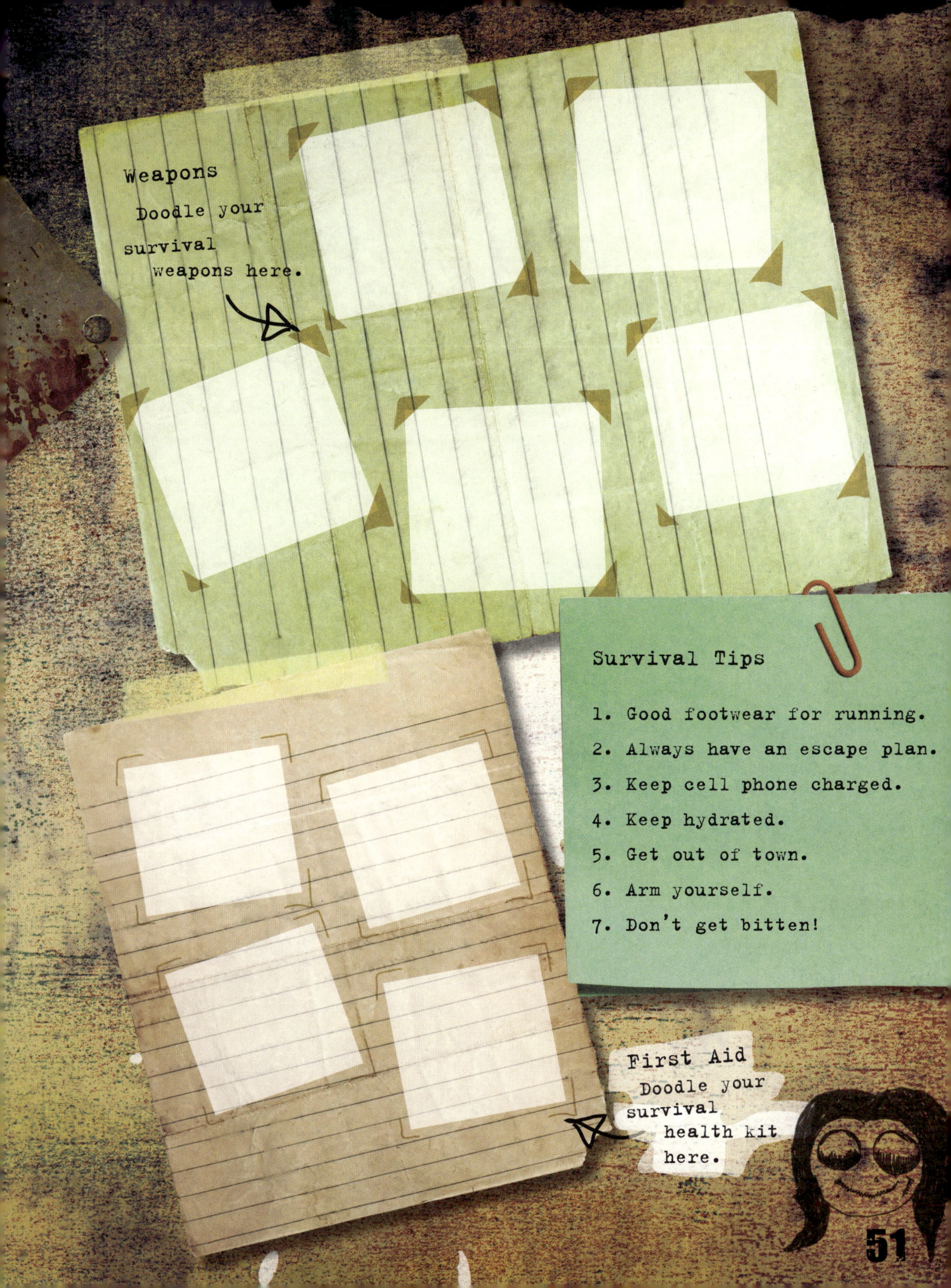
Weapons
Doodle your survival weapons here.
Survival Tips
1. Good footwear for running.
2. Always have an escape plan.
3. Keep cell phone charged.
4. Keep hydrated.
5. Get out of town.
6. Arm yourself.
7. Don't get bitten!
First Aid
Doodle your survival health kit here.

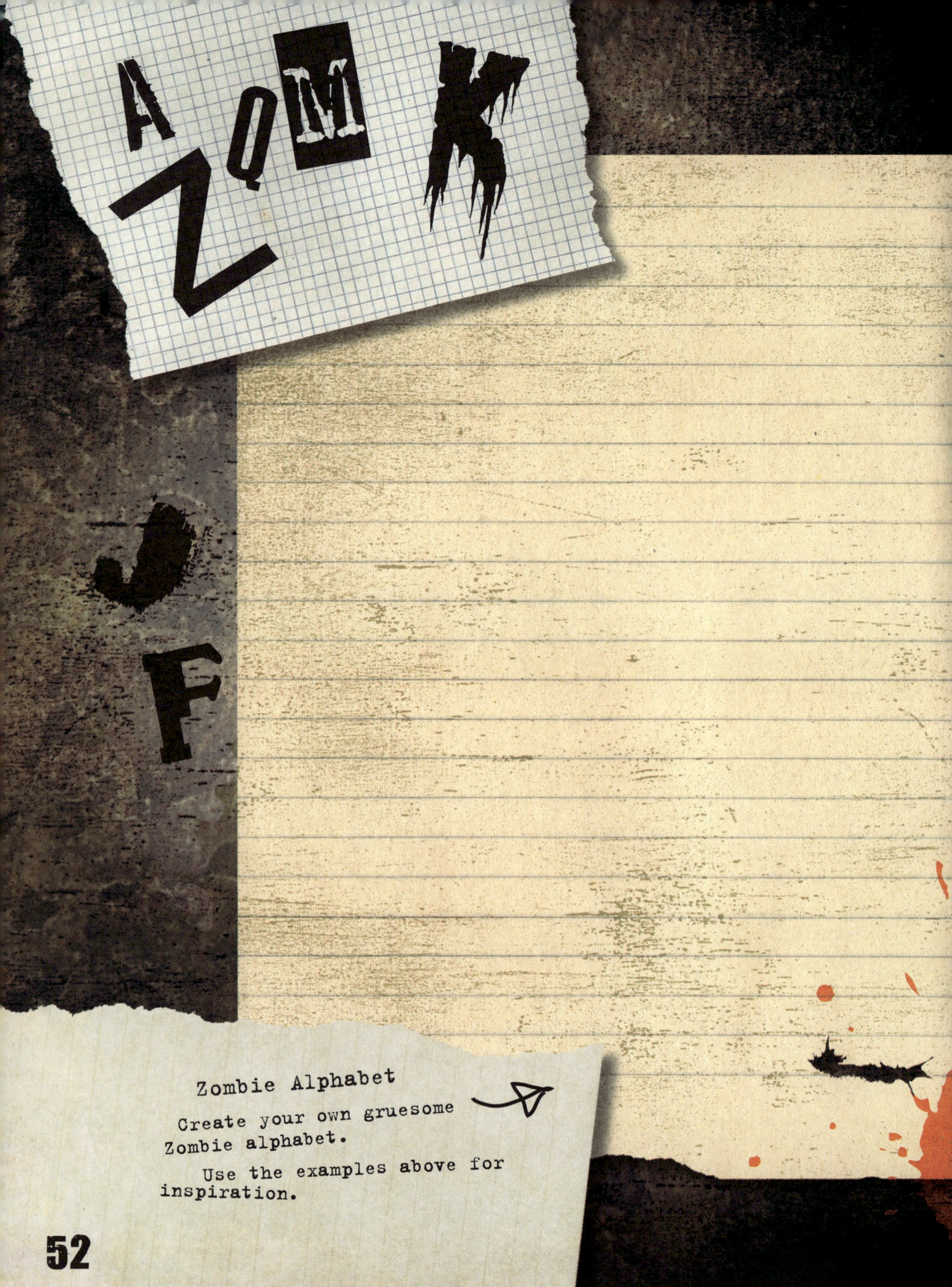

Zombie Alphabet

Create your own gruesome Zombie alphabet.

Use the examples above for inspiration.

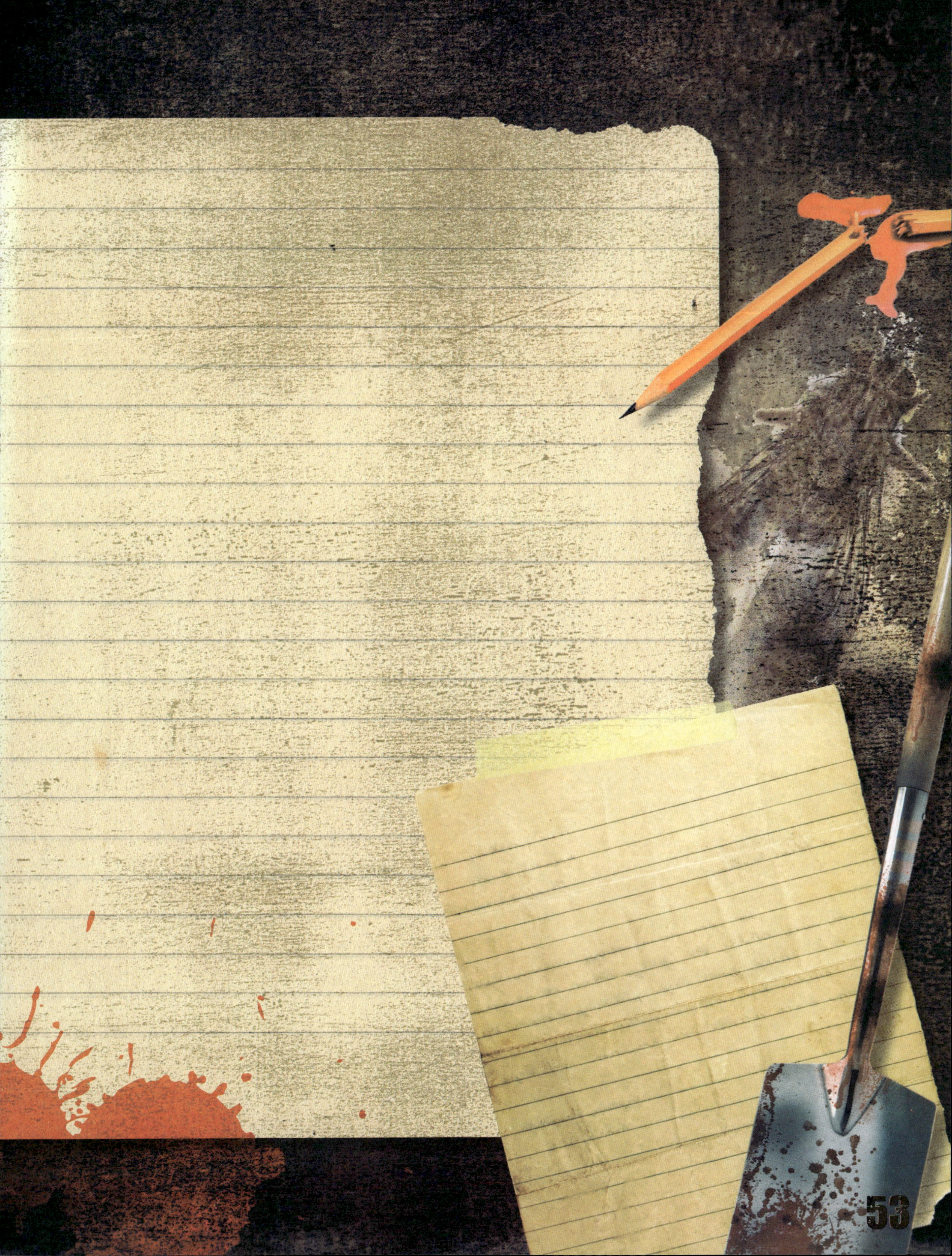

WORD SEARCH 3

h	s	s	i	i	u	e	a	y	s
t	k	i	d	n	e	y	s	c	u
i	i	c	e	e	e	a	o	n	t
m	u	s	c	l	e	s	e	h	o
o	s	e	i	r	e	t	r	a	n
v	s	v	c	s	o	o	n	a	g
t	e	n	i	p	a	m	o	i	u
r	a	u	i	t	r	a	e	h	e
p	r	p	r	e	v	c	t	a	n
b	t	s	u	n	v	h	e	c	h

arteries	liver	throat
bruises	muscles	tongue
heart	pancreas	veins
kidneys	stomach	vomit

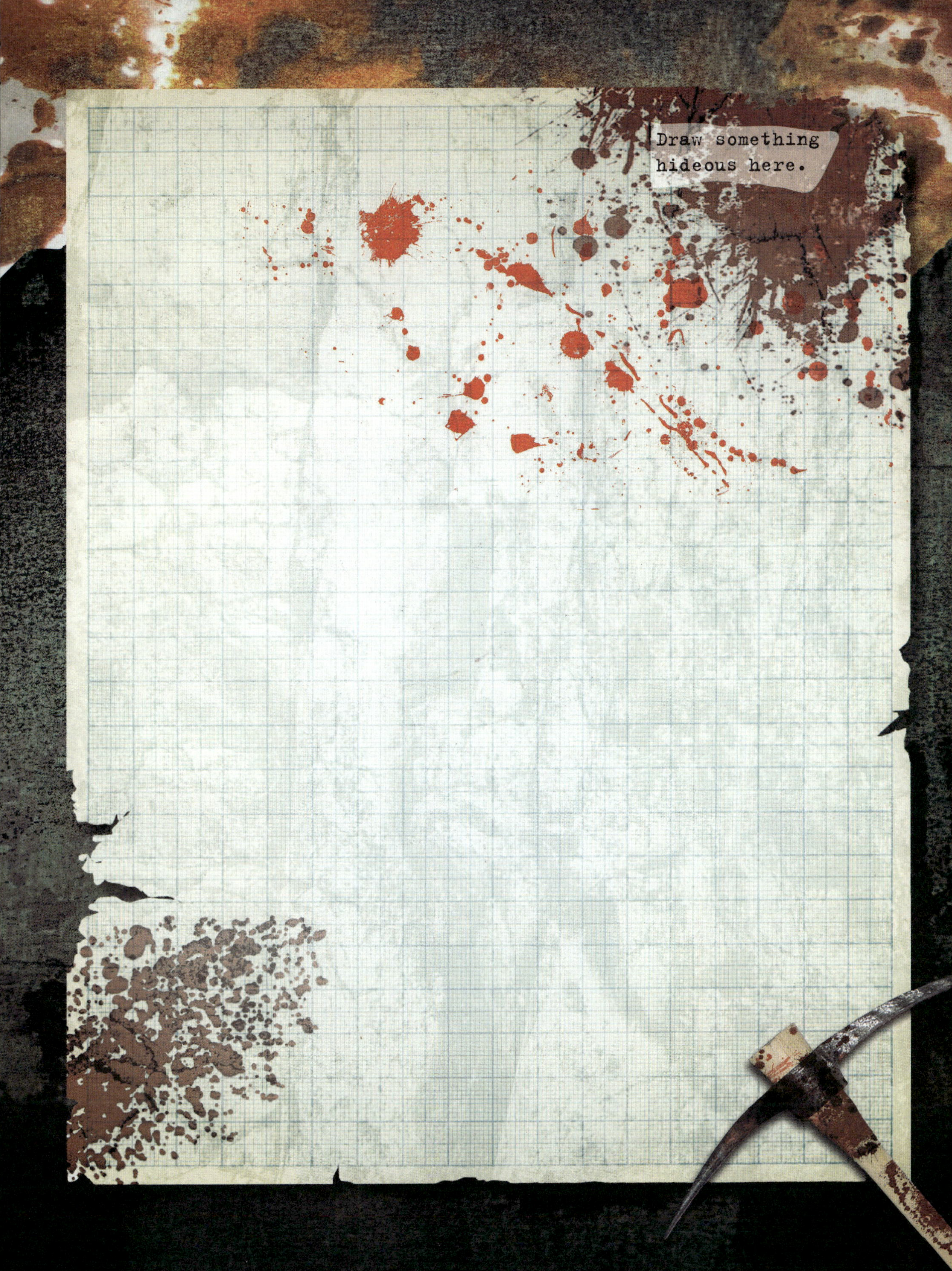
Draw something
hideous here.

WALK THE LINE

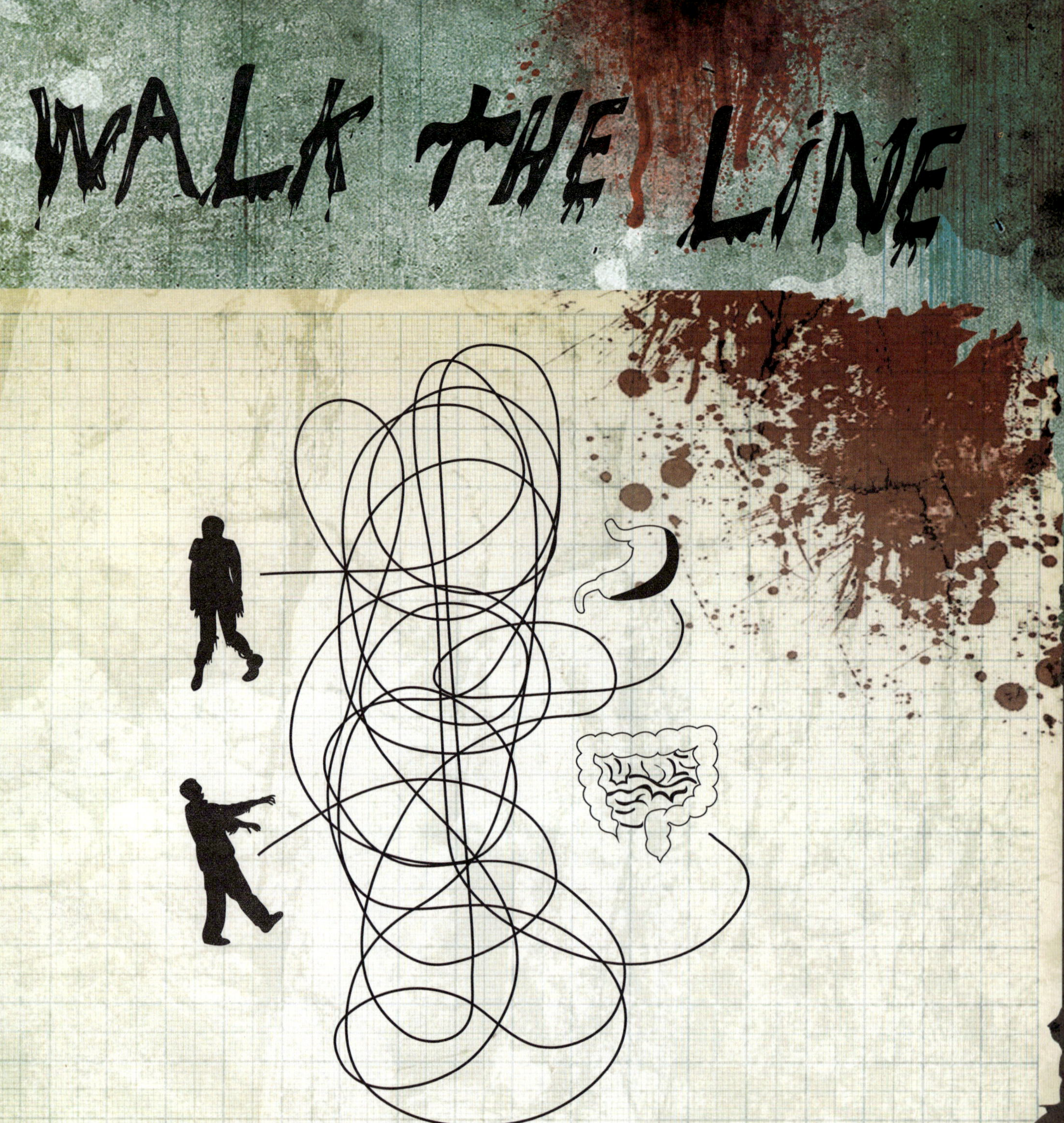

Discover which zombie will feed on the lovely guts and intestine or rancid stomach lining by following their only lifelines.

Your friend has been bitten by a hungry zombie. Write their obituary here.

"I'll swallow your soul, I'll swallow your soul!!!"

Evil Dead II

ZOMBIE HANGMAN

Cross off the dead letters.

ABCDEFGHIJKLMNOPQRSTUVWXYZ

Draw your hangman.

Enter your blood-soaked words here.

ABCDEFG
HIJKLM
NOPQRST
UVWXYZ

Cross off the dead letters.

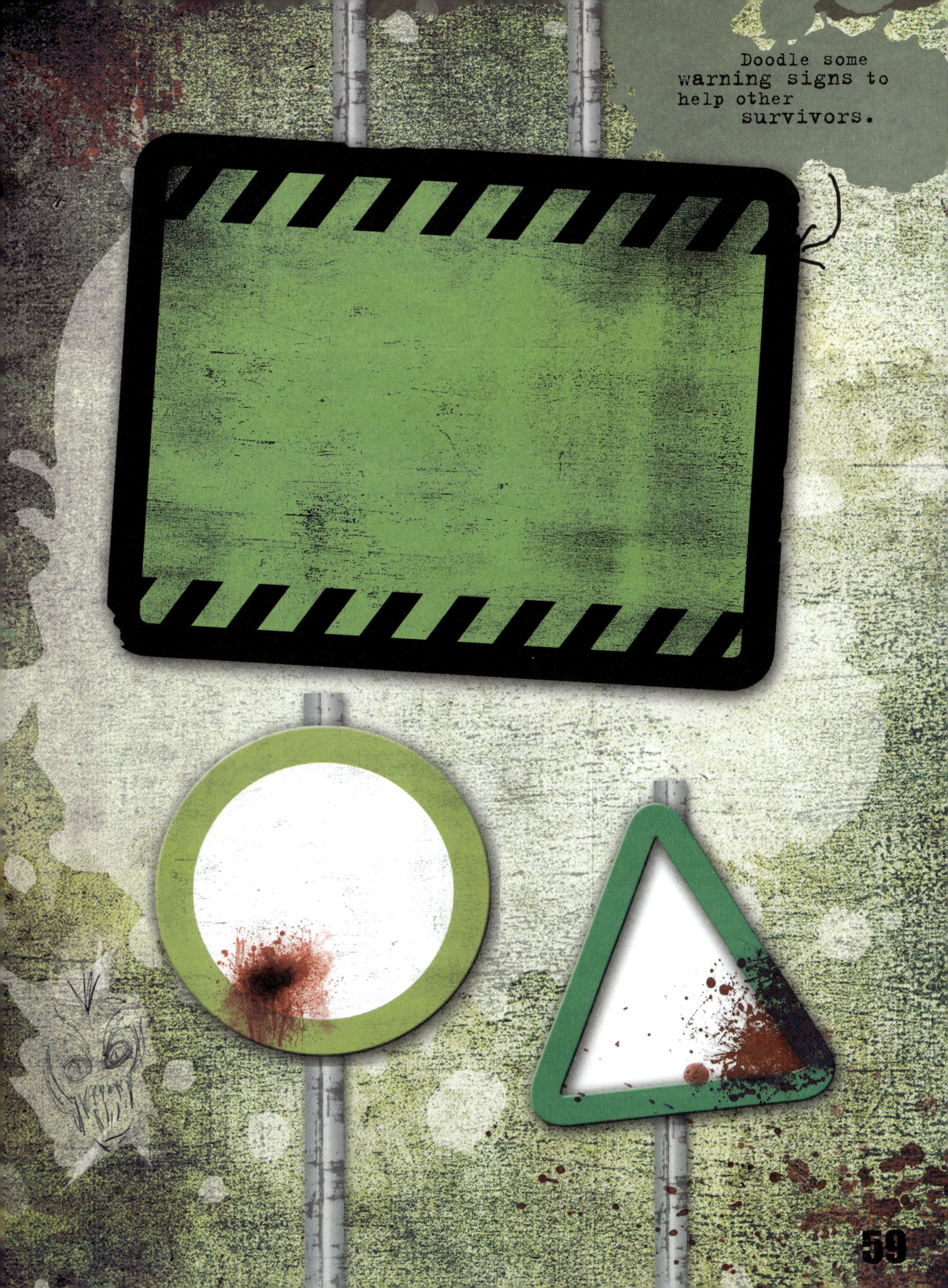
Doodle some
warning signs to
help other
survivors.

CONNECT THE ~~ZOMBIES~~ DOTS

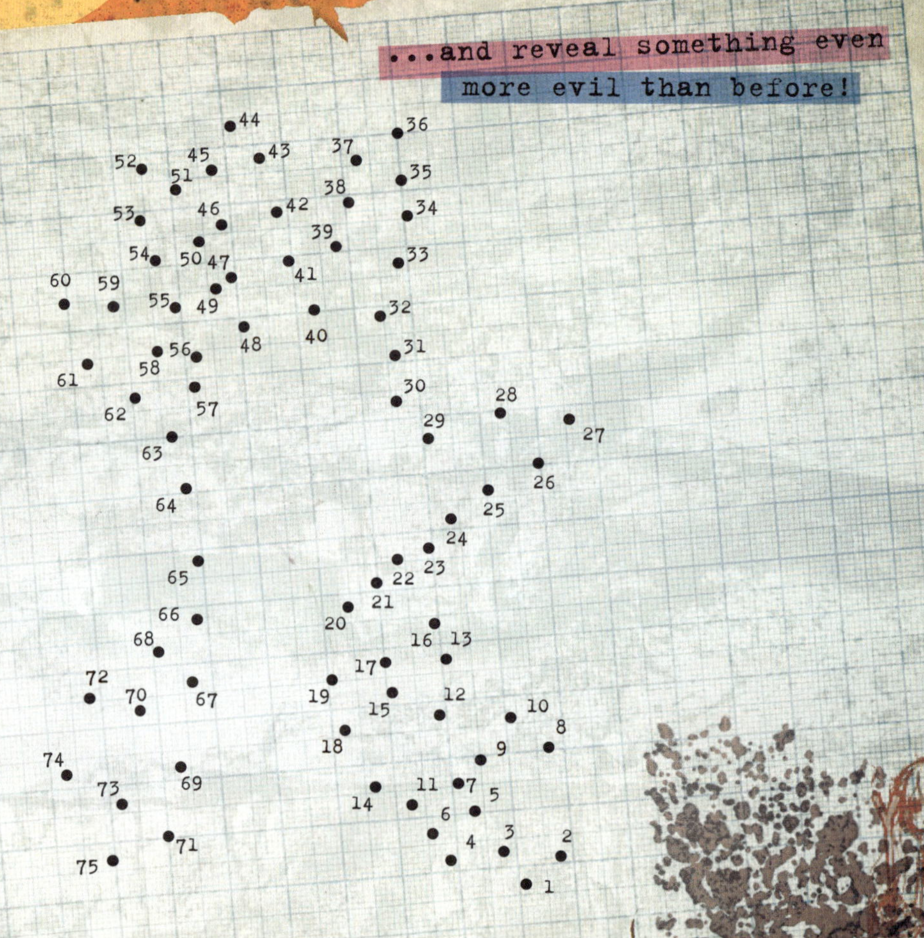

"YOUR MOTHER ATE MY DOG!"

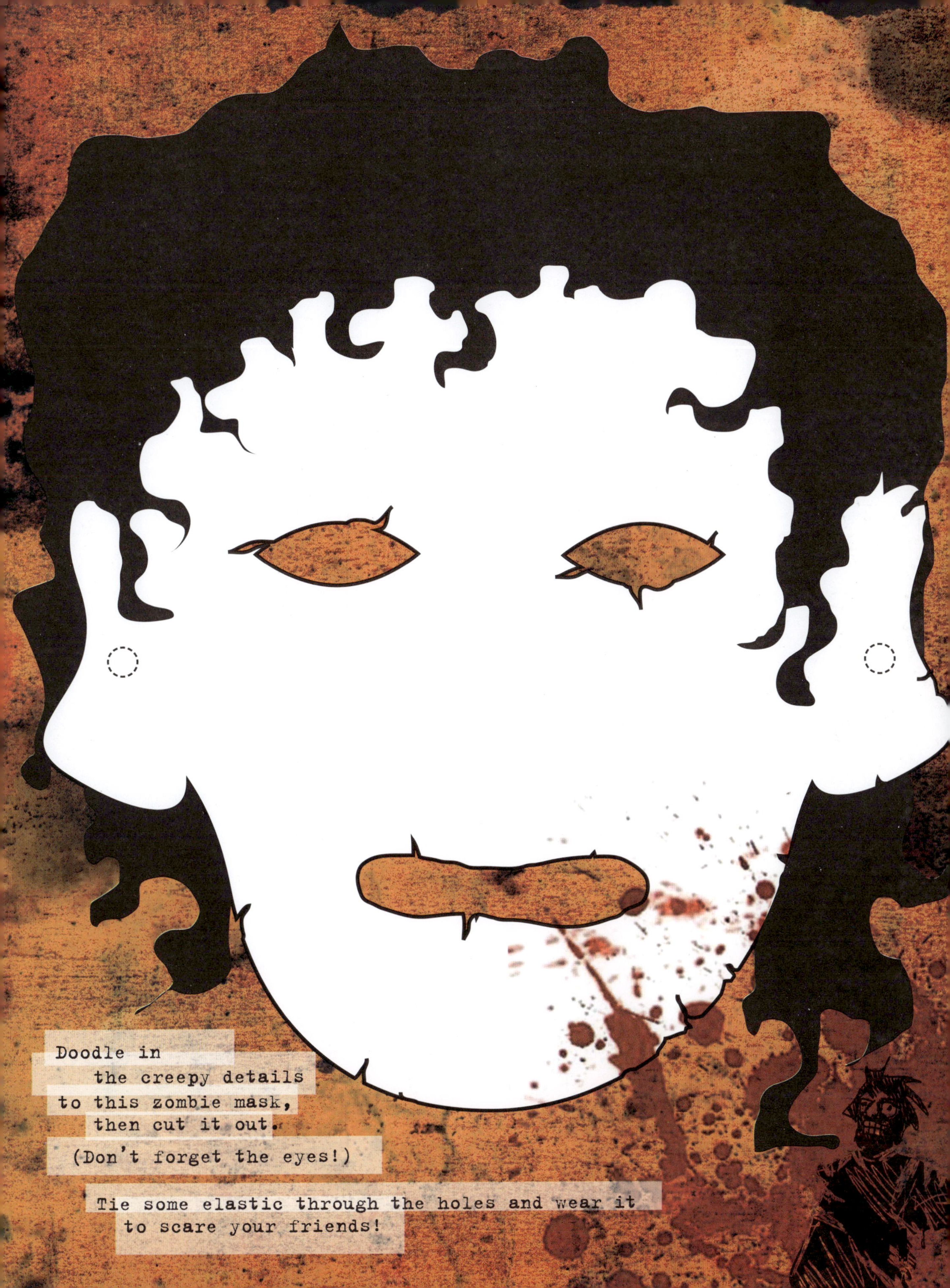

Doodle in
the creepy details
to this zombie mask,
then cut it out.
(Don't forget the eyes!)
Tie some elastic through the holes and wear it
to scare your friends!

Place your mirror here to reveal the sinister message.

BRAIN DEAD

Write an evil message backward and view it in the mirror. Use some creepy fonts for a scary effect!

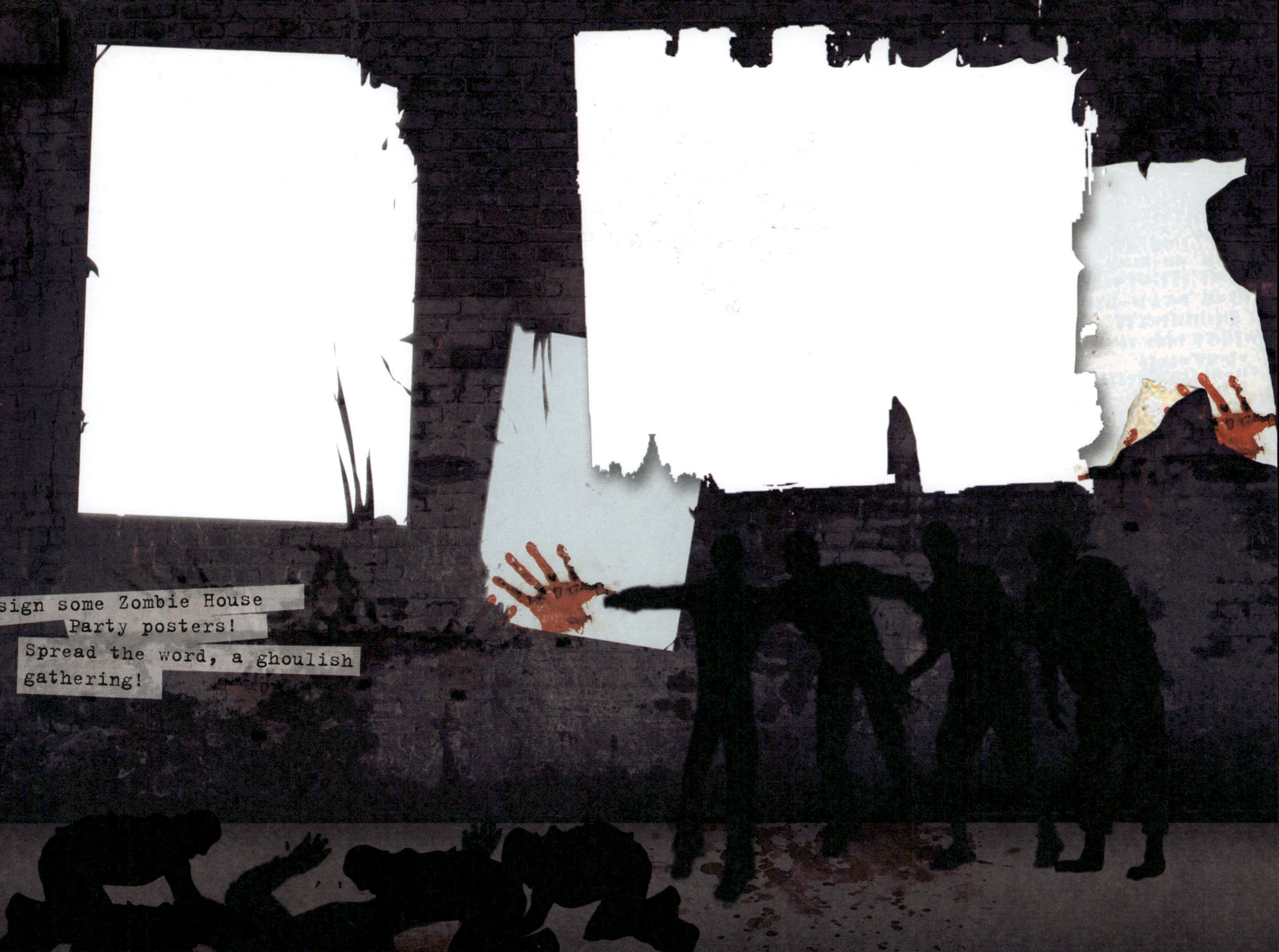
sign some Zombie House
Party posters!
Spread the word, a ghoulish
gathering!

SPOT THE DIFFERENCE

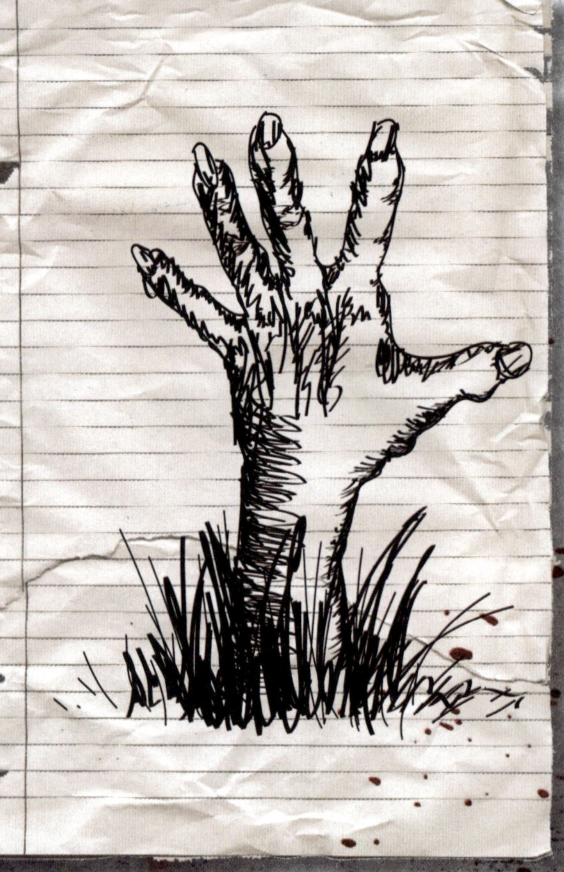

Can you spot the 5 differences between these 2 zombie hands?

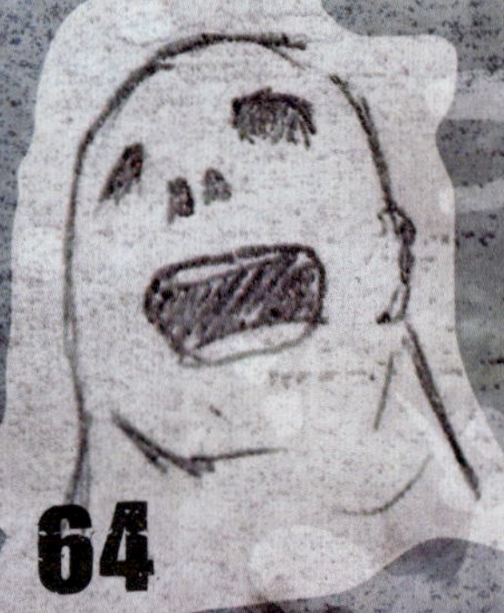

"You told, you told, now you die like me."

RETURN OF THE *LIVING* DEAD PART II

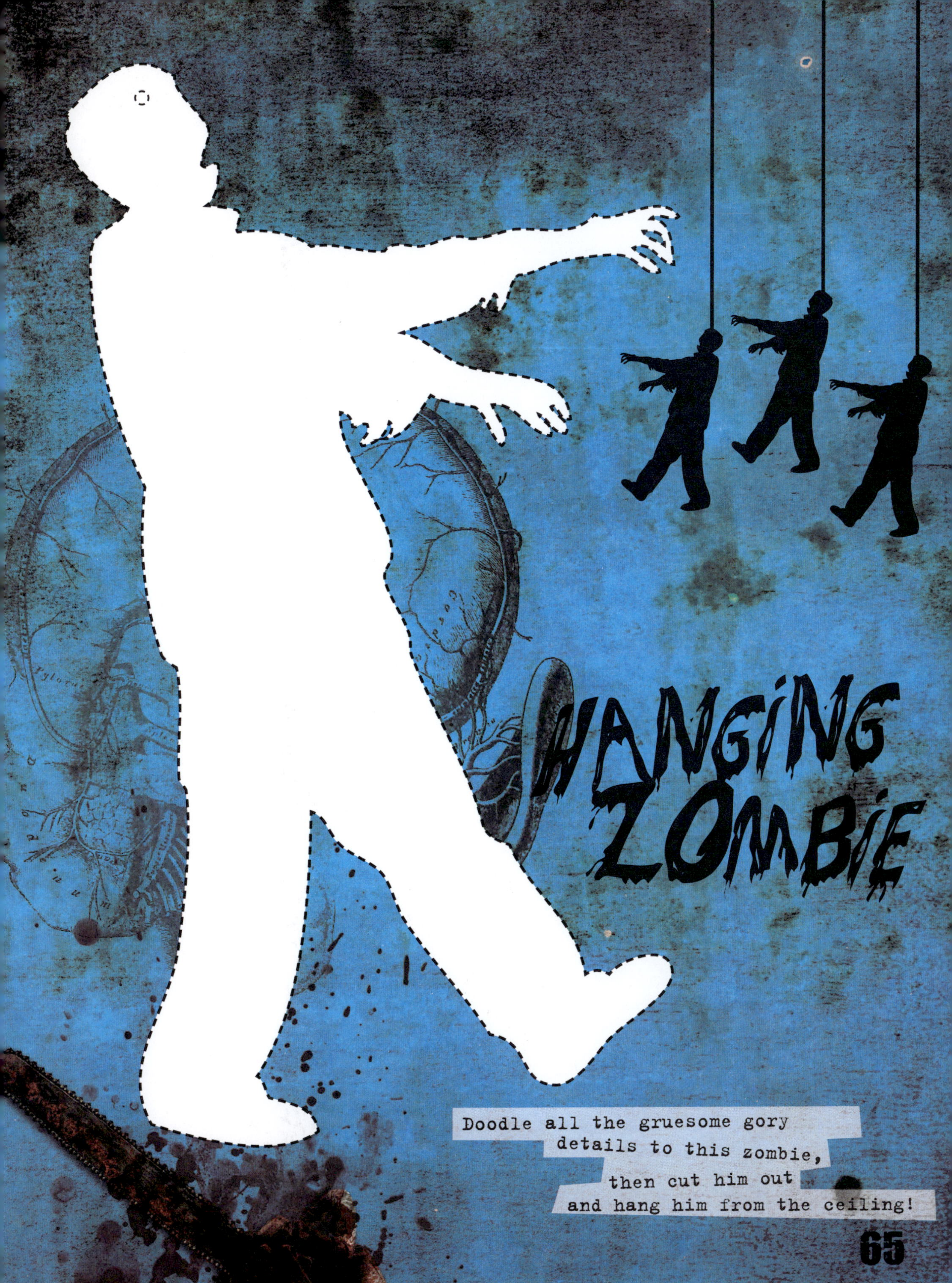

HANGING ZOMBIE

Doodle all the gruesome gory details to this zombie, then cut him out and hang him from the ceiling!

Cut out the stencil,
doodle an image into this blood splatter stencil,
and cut out.
For example:
a skull or a biohazard symbol.

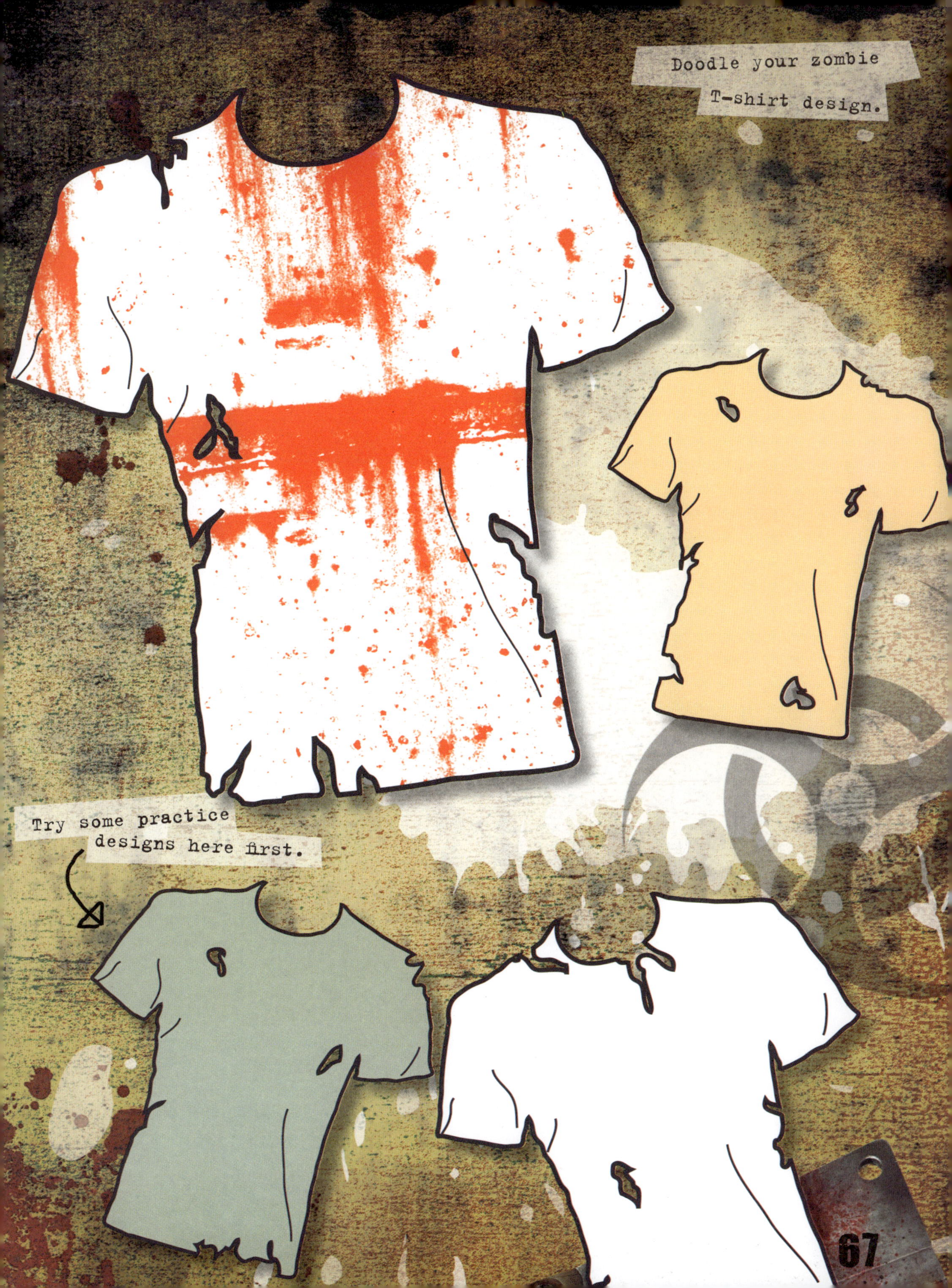
Doodle your zombie
T-shirt design.
Try some practice
designs here first.

HELL'S SOUP

Ingredients

1 lb. raw beets, well washed

1 tbsp. olive oil

2 onions, peeled and sliced

1 clove garlic, peeled and crushed

1 tsp. chili powder

1/2 tbsp. tomato purée

2 x 14 oz. cans chopped tomatoes

salt and pepper

herby garlic bread, to serve

Warning adult assistance recommended for a safe result!

Method

1. Heat the oven to 400F. Wrap the beets individually in foil and bake in the oven until tender, about 1 hour. Cool, peel, and dice into 1/2-in pieces.

2. Heat the oil in a large saucepan and add the onions and the garlic. Cook for 2-3 minutes until it starts to soften. Add the chili powder and cook for another minute. Add the tomato purée and cans of chopped tomatoes, season well, and bring to a boil. Lower the heat and simmer for 15 minutes.

3. Liquidize the soup and add more water if you prefer it thinner. Stir in the beet cubes, heat through, and serve with herby garlic bread.

Doodle in the
sleeping zombie.

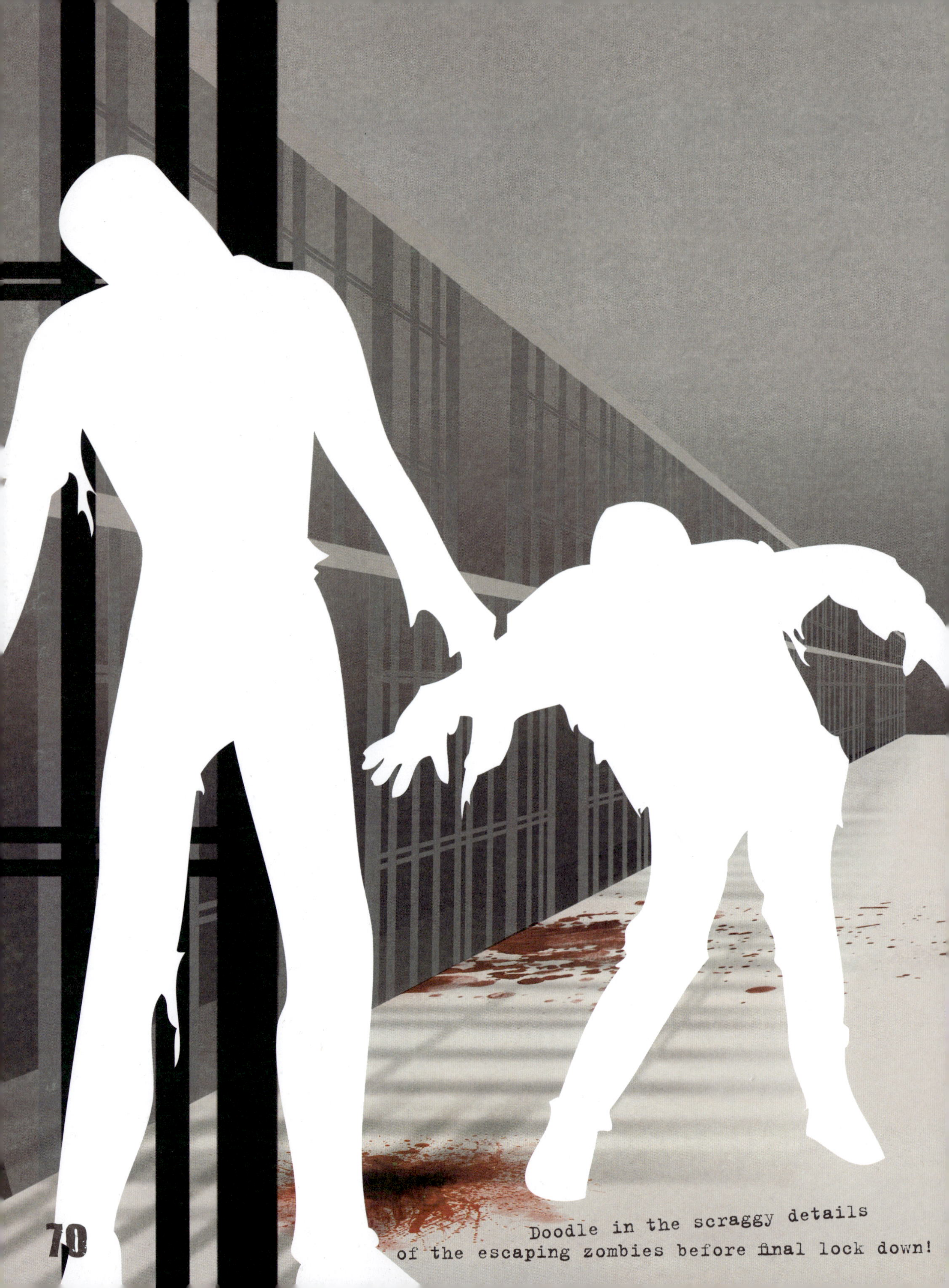

Doodle in the scraggy details
of the escaping zombies before final lock down!

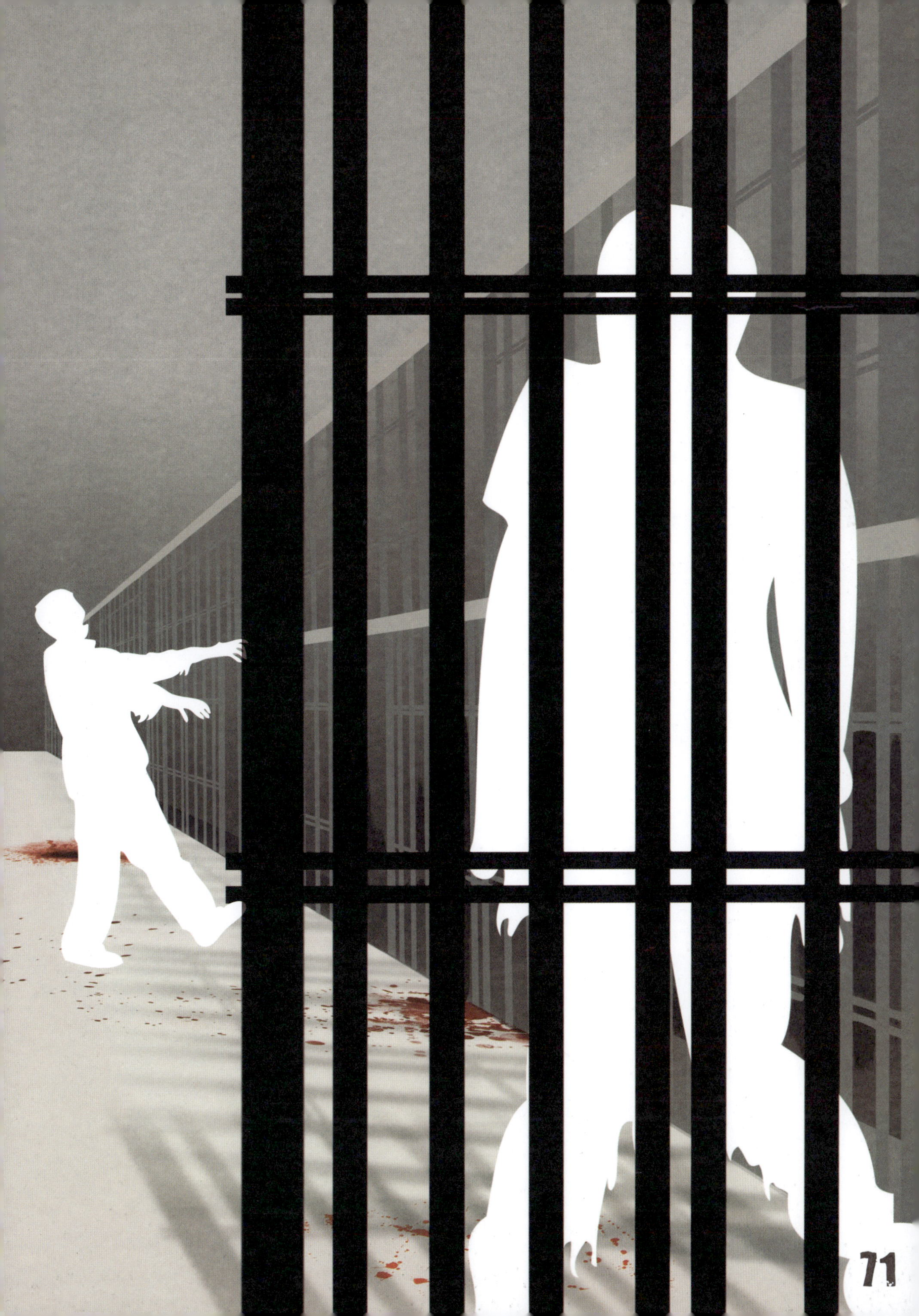

Doodle and design some zombie greetings cards.

"You see? You just can't trust anyone. The first girl I let into my life and she tries to eat me."

ZOMBIELAND

Some can be
hideous
and gross.
Or try something
funny and
witty.

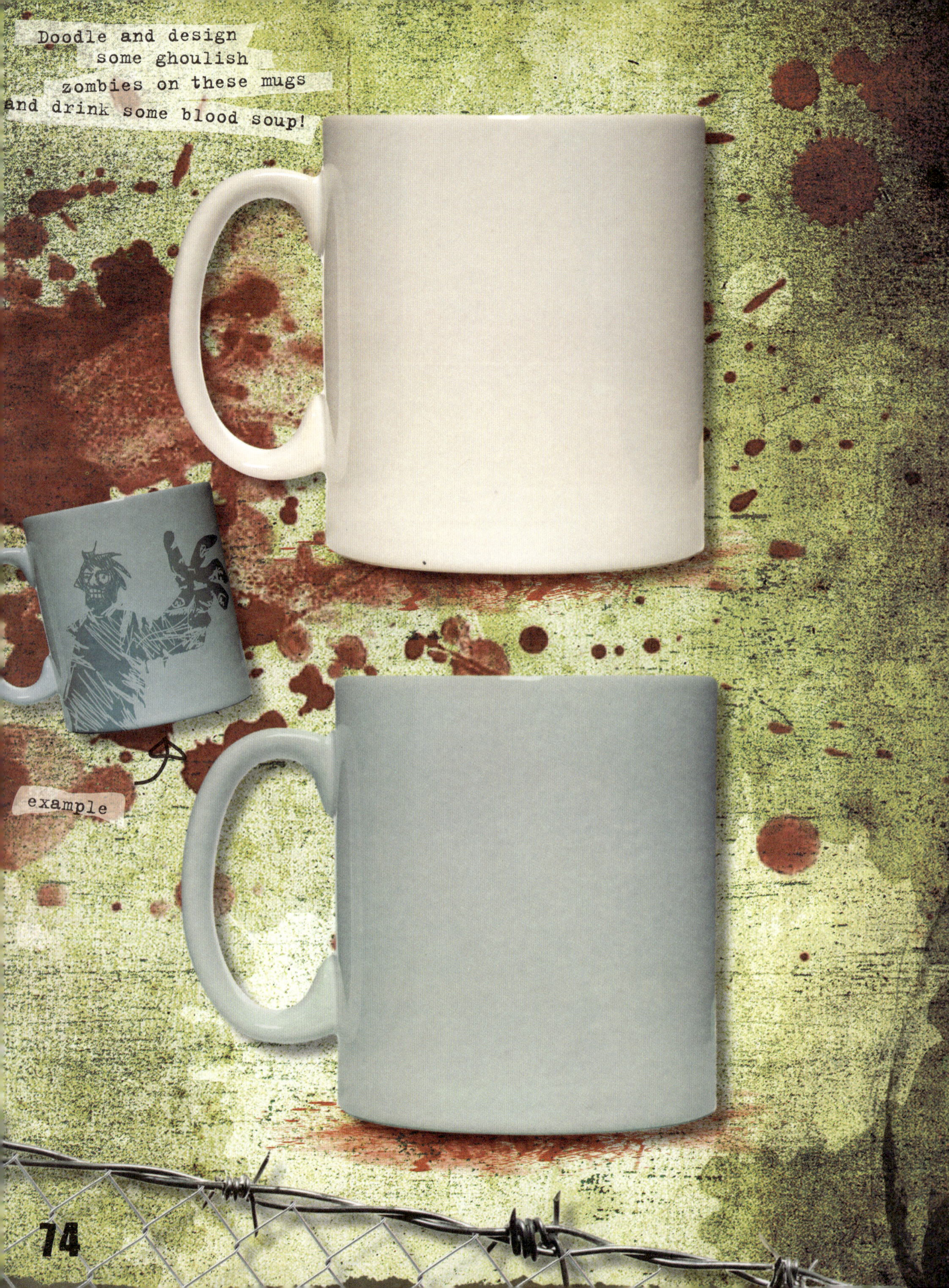
Doodle and design
some ghoulish
zombies on these mugs
and drink some blood soup!
example

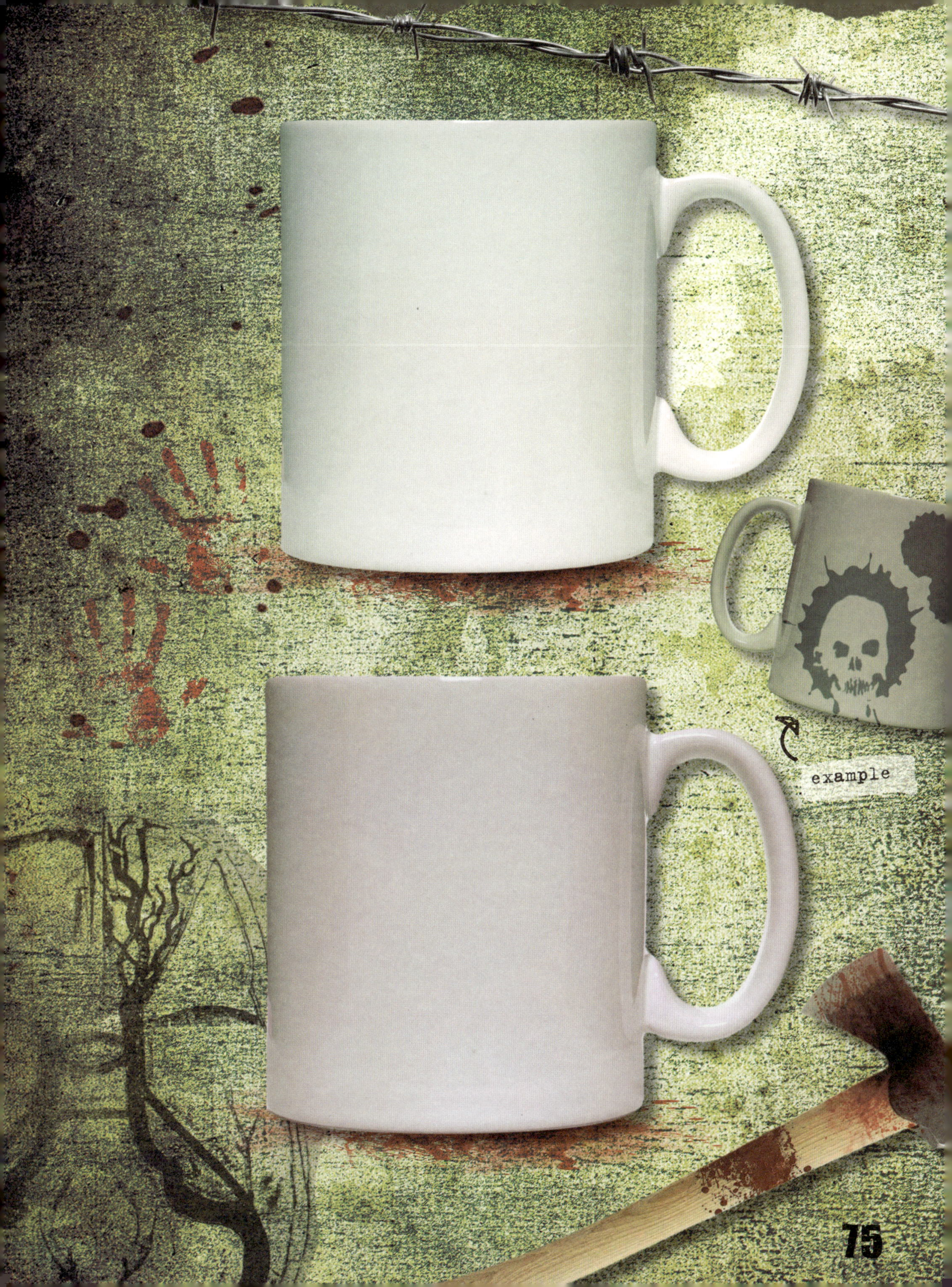
example

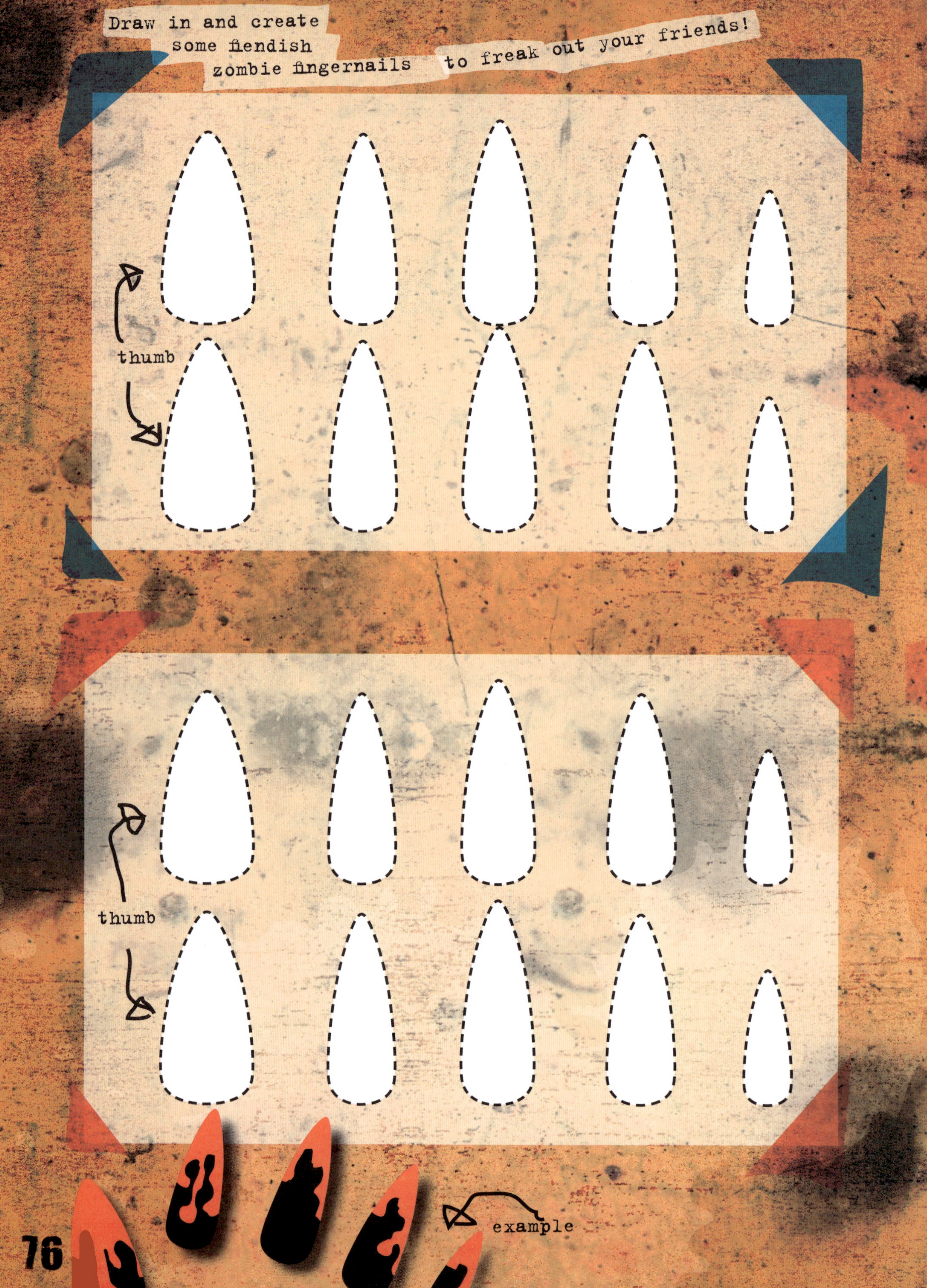
Draw in and create
some fiendish
zombie fingernails
to freak out your friends!
thumb
thumb
example

Design your very own organ donor card. If you're going to donate, why not give to the zombies!

example

organ donor card

I WOULD LIKE MY ORGANS DONATED TO THE ZOMBIE FOODATION

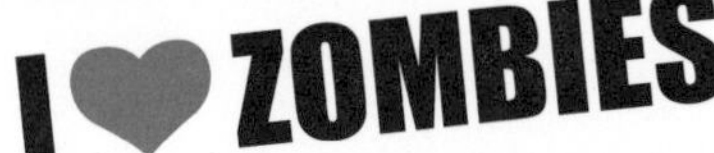

I ❤ ZOMBIES

THE EXTRAS WHO PLAYED THE ZOMBIES WERE PAID $1 AND GIVEN A T-SHIRT THAT SAID "I WAS A ZOMBIE ON NIGHT OF THE LIVING DEAD."

WORD SEARCH 4

o b l i t e r a t i o n e
s i p l e e n n n e l a s
e x t e r m i n a t i o n
l c r p m a g i p t f a y
a t a i i s h h o e e r d
m e d d n s t i c d l m o
e a y e a a m l a e e a o
n r s m t c a a l s s g m
t s t i i r r t y o s e i
e a o c o e e i p l a d n
d e p y n p l o s a e d a
m m i o s i m n e t t o a
s l a u g h t e r e d n d

annihilation
apocalypse
armageddon
desolate
doom
dystopia
epidemic
extermination
lamented
lifeless
massacre
nightmare
obliteration
slaughtered
termination

Draw something
hideous here.

SHORT DEAD LINES

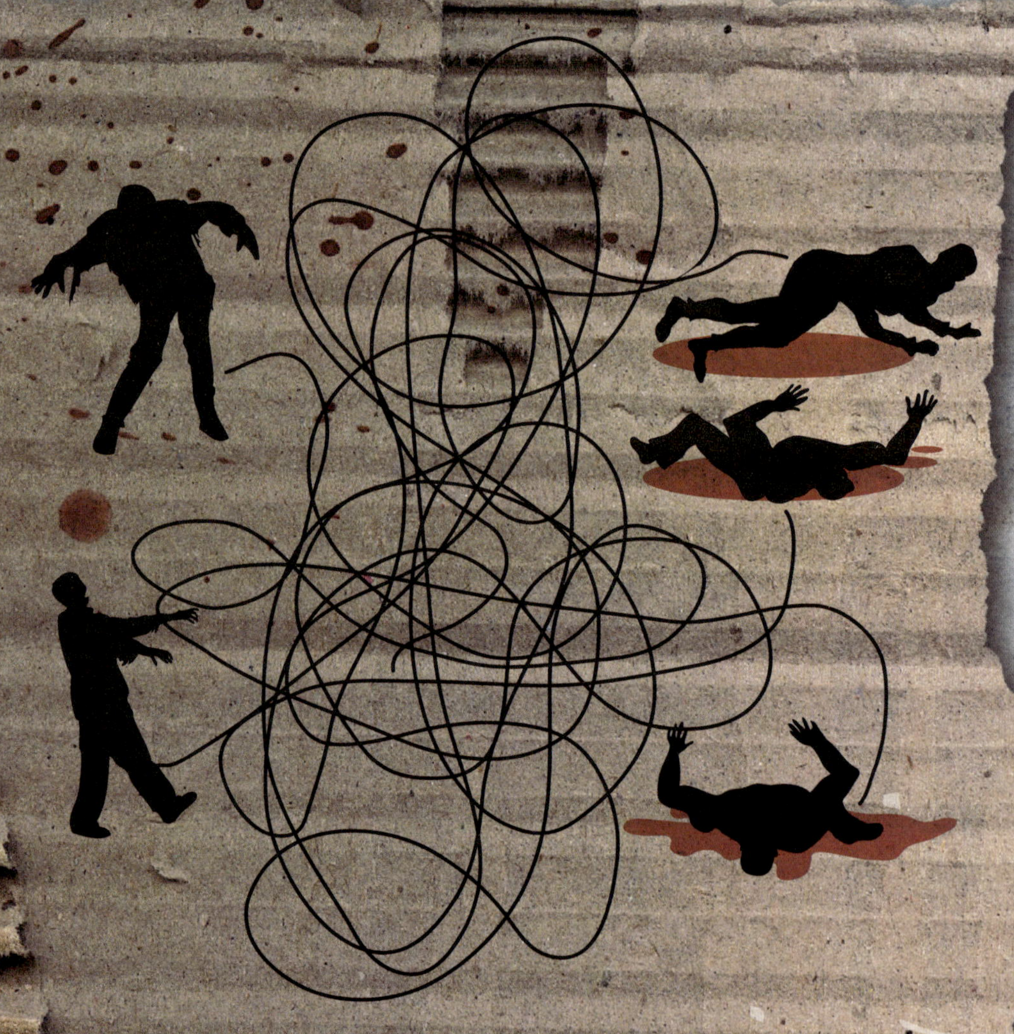

The two zombies choose their victims wisely, follow the tangled lines to discover who got away!

Zombie Trap

There's been a break-through! A cure for the zombie virus has been found!

Doodle a cunning plan to trap a zombie for the testing to begin.

Good luck!

George A. Romero—"Godfather of all zombies" and creator of DAWN OF THE DEAD—was so impressed with Simon Pegg and Edgar Wright's work in their spoof SHAUN OF THE DEAD that he asked them to appear in LAND OF THE DEAD, the fourth part of his Dead series, in cameos as zombies.

ZOMBIE HANGMAN

Cross off the dead letters.

ABCDEFGHIJKLMNOPQRSTUVWXYZ

Draw your hangman.

Enter your blood-soaked words here.

_ _ _

ABCDEFG
HIJKLM
NOPQRST
UVWXYZ

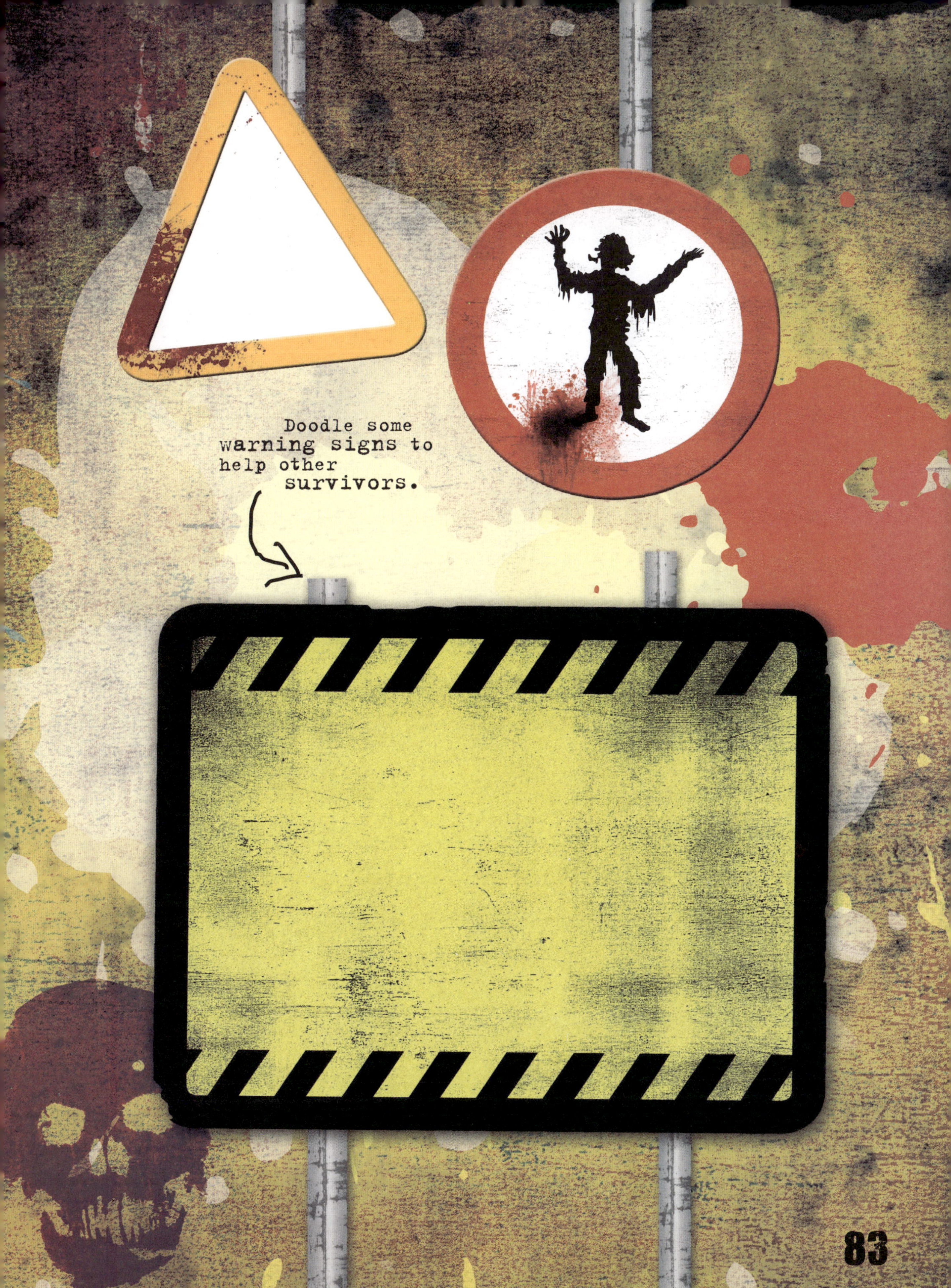
Doodle some
warning signs to
help other
survivors.

CONNECT THE ~~ZOMBIES~~ DOTS

... and reveal the final cut!

28 DAYS LATER: Revealing mistakes: In the opening scenes where Jim is standing at the steps at the bottom of steps on the junction of Carlton House Terrace and Waterloo Place (after leaving the hospital) you can clearly see a person walking down the hill on the right hand side.

ZOMBIE QUIZ

1. Who directed the zombie portion of the recent movie GRINDHOUSE (2007)?
   A: Joss Whedon
   B: Eli Roth
   C: Robert Rodriguez

2. Largely considered the first zombie film, WHITE ZOMBIE (1932) starred which horror stalwart?
   A: Bela Lugosi
   B: Boris Karloff
   C: Henry Daniell

3. Who wrote the book and screenplay PET SEMATARY, which became a film about zombie animals and children?
   A: Dean R. Koontz
   B: Stephen King
   C: Clive Barker

4. Name George A. Romero's first full-length zombie film.
   A: DAWN OF THE DEAD
   B: DAY OF THE DEAD
   C: NIGHT OF THE LIVING DEAD

5. In SHAUN OF THE DEAD (2004), what was the song playing on the jukebox when the central characters were attacking the zombie pub landlord?
   A: "Pinball Wizard" by The Who
   B: "Hey Ya" by Outkast
   C: "Don't Stop Me Now" by Queen

ZOMBIE QUIZ (continued)

6. Which film started life as a zombie computer game?
   A: RESIDENT EVIL
   B: PUPPET MASTER
   C: THE EVIL DEAD

7. What does the acronym CHUD stand for from the 1983 camp horror and its sequel, CHUD II?
   A: CADAVER HUNTING UNFROZEN DUDES
   B: CANNIBALISTIC HUMANOID UNDERGROUND DWELLER
   C: CANNIBALS HAVE UNLEASHED DEATH

8. PET SEMATARY II (1992) saw which former ER TV doctor take the lead role?
   A: Anthony Edwards
   B: George Clooney
   C: Eriq La Salle

9. Which actress played the lead role in the teen flick ZOMBIE HIGH (1987)?
   A: Kirstie Alley
   B: Virginia Madsen
   C: Shannen Doherty

10. PLAN 9 FROM OUTER SPACE—often dubbed the worst movie ever made—was directed by which Hollywood eccentric?
    A: Stanley Kubrick
    B: Ed Wood Jr.
    C: John Waters

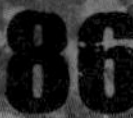

Design some zombie rock venue
music posters!
Let's get the monster mash
going!

SPOT THE DIFFERENCE

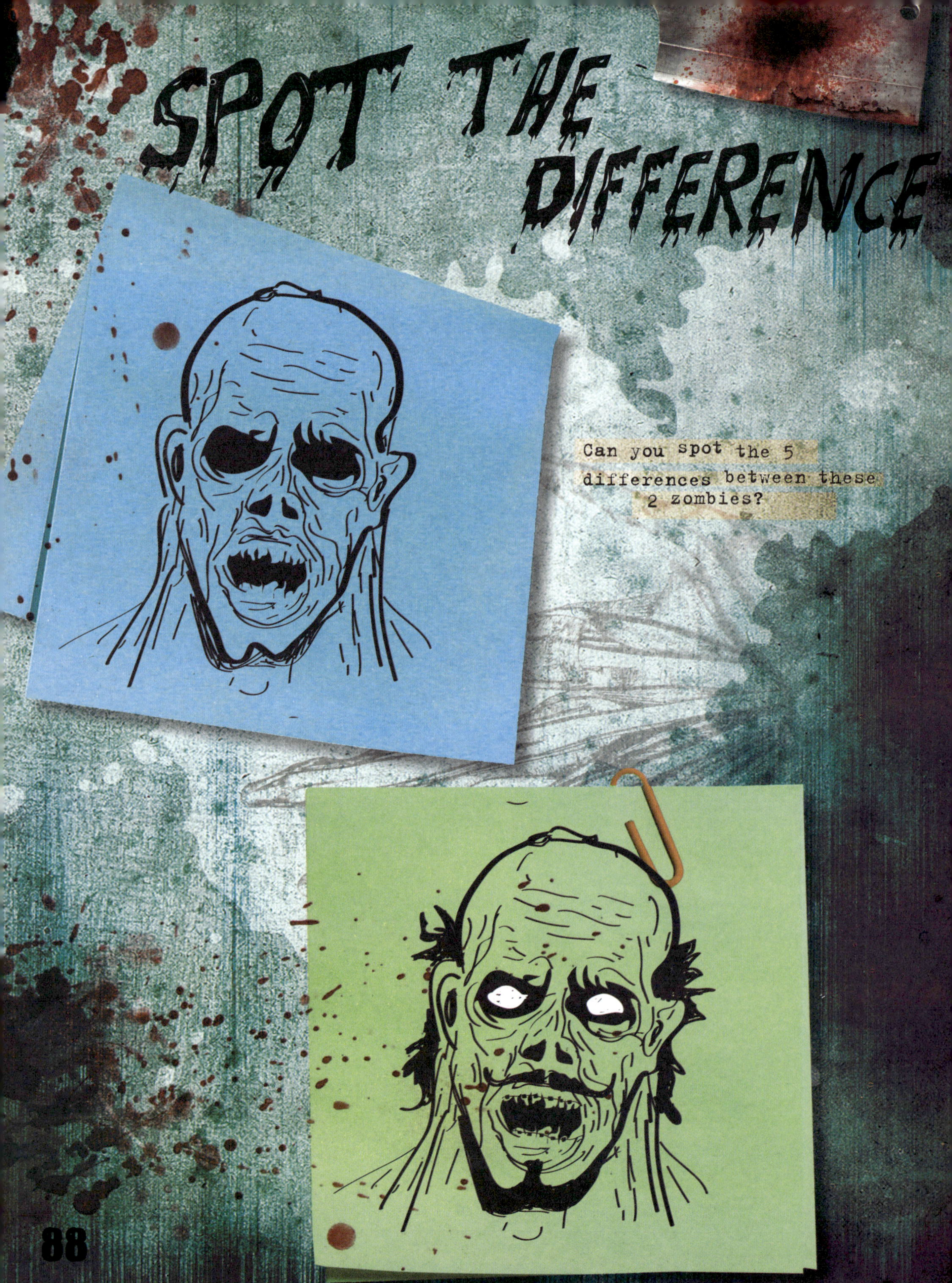

Can you spot the 5 differences between these 2 zombies?

Zombie Trap

The first trap worked!

Well done! We need more test subjects; doodle and design more traps. The world depends on it!

WHERE DO ZOMBIES GO SWIMMING?

THE DEAD SEA

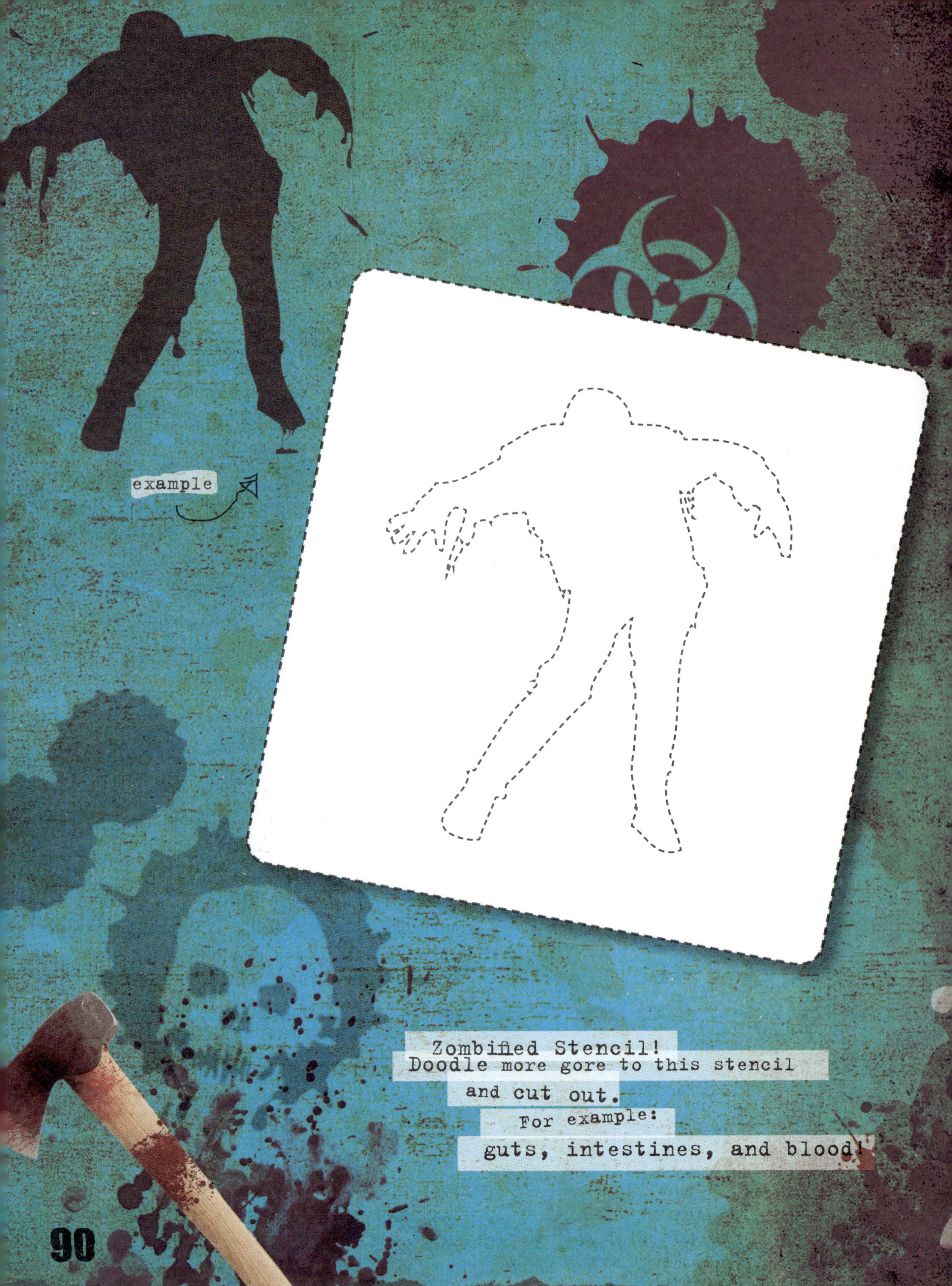

Zombified Stencil!
Doodle more gore to this stencil
and cut out.
For example:
guts, intestines, and blood!

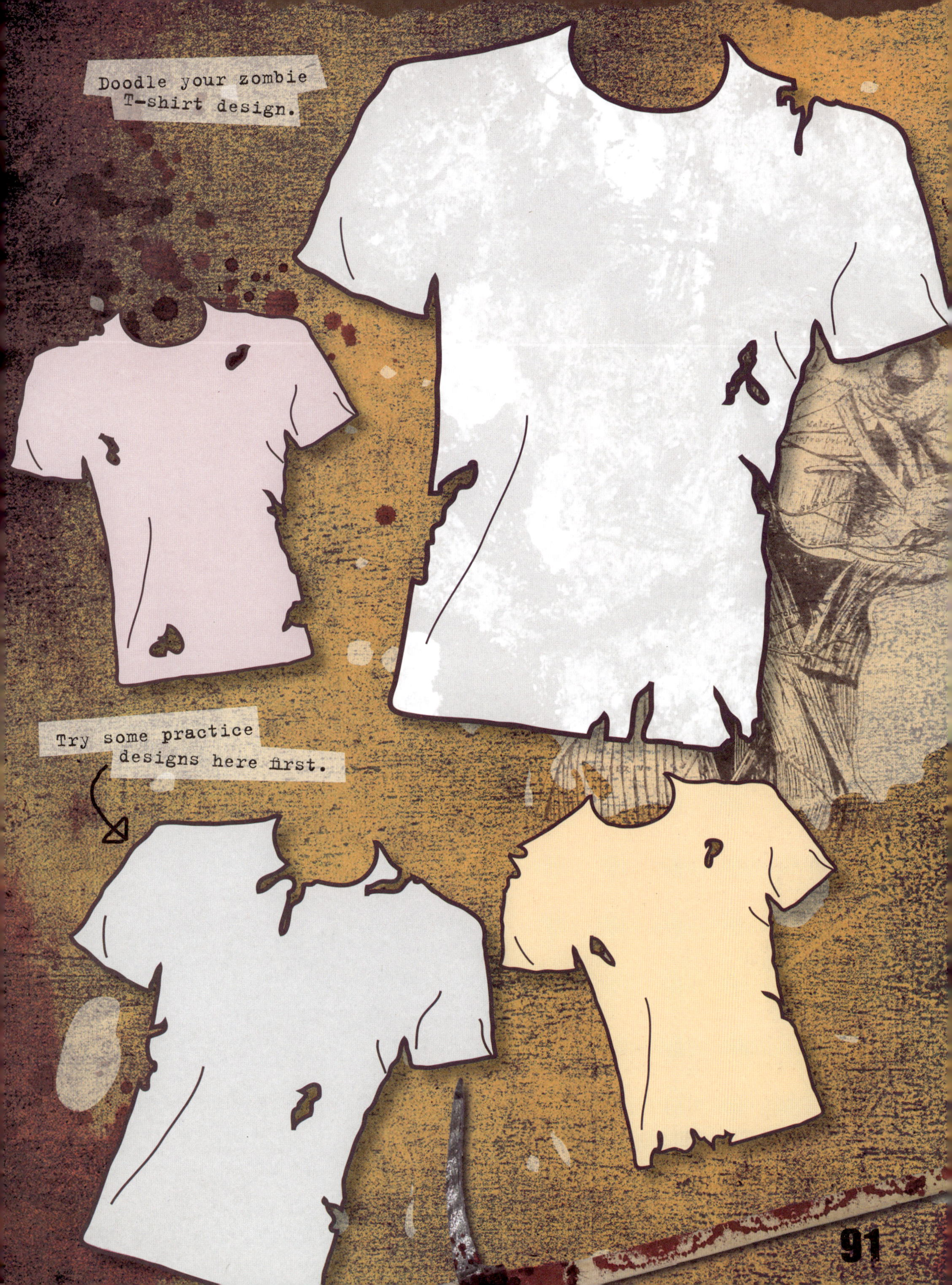
Doodle your zombie T-shirt design.
Try some practice designs here first.

EYEBALL CAKE

Ingredients

4 oz. margarine
6 oz. sugar
14 oz. dried fruit—this can be a mixture of raisins, sultanas, cherries, peel, etc.
8 fl. oz. water
1 tsp. baking soda
$^{1}/_{2}$ tsp. mixed spice
2 beaten eggs
4 oz. all-purpose flour
4 oz. self-rising Flour
Pinch of salt

Method

1. Preheat the oven to 350 degrees.
2. Prepare the pan by applying a thin layer of margarine and lining with 2 layers of parchment paper.
3. Put the margarine, sugar, fruit, water, baking soda, and mixed spice in a saucepan over medium heat. Bring to a boil and simmer for 1 minute.
4. Pour into a mixing bowl and let cool.
5. Add eggs, flour, and salt to cooled mixture. Mix well and pour into prepared pan.
6. Bake for about 1 hour 15 minutes. You may need to put brown paper over the top if the cake starts to singe before it is cooked throughout. The cke is ready when an inserted skewer comes out clean. Let cool on a wire rack.

Warning
adult assistance
recommended for a
safe result!

Making the eyeball

You need...

White icing

Red gel icing

Food coloring

Directions

1. To make your own version of this Halloween cake, sculpt a round eyeball shape out of stacked layer cakes, or use a 3-D ball-shaped pan to make the cake.
2. Tint frosting to your desired eyeball colors as in the picture, and create the same eyeball design.
3. Draw the squiggly red lines to give it a spooky touch!

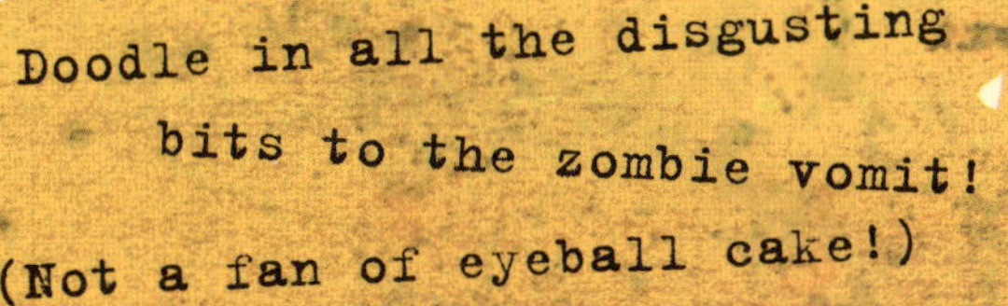

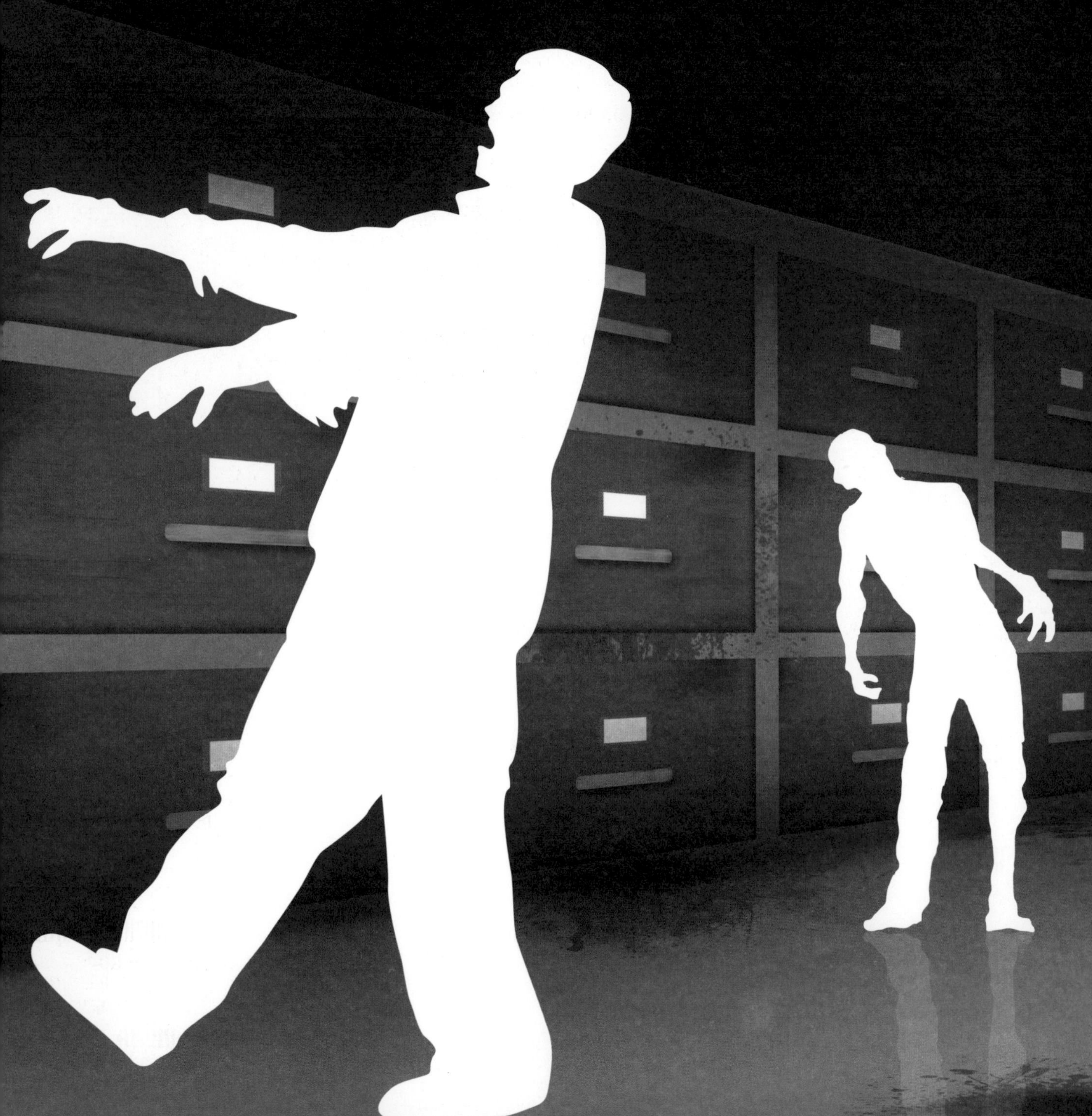

Doodle in the bloody details
to this flesh hungry zombie scene.

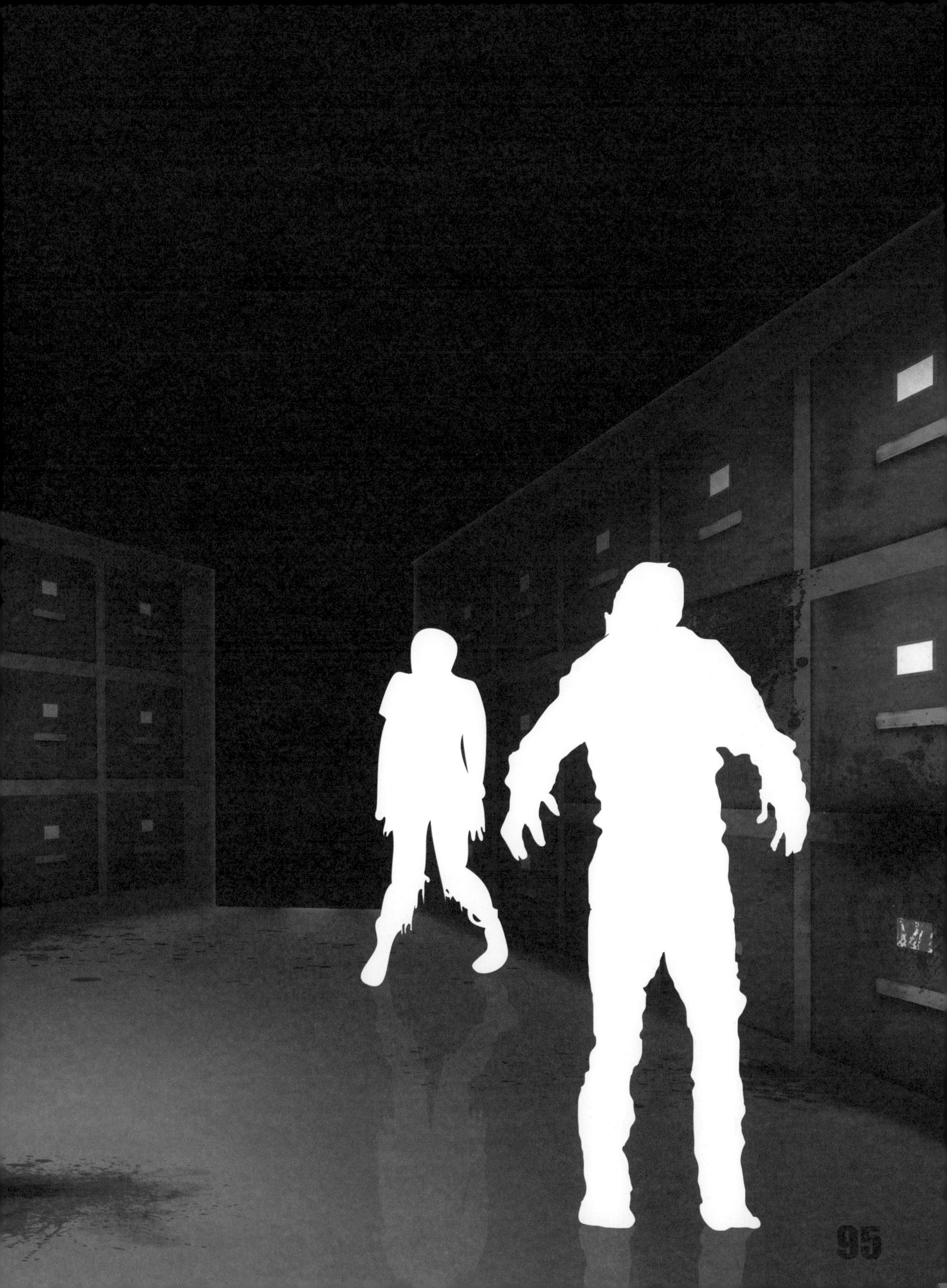

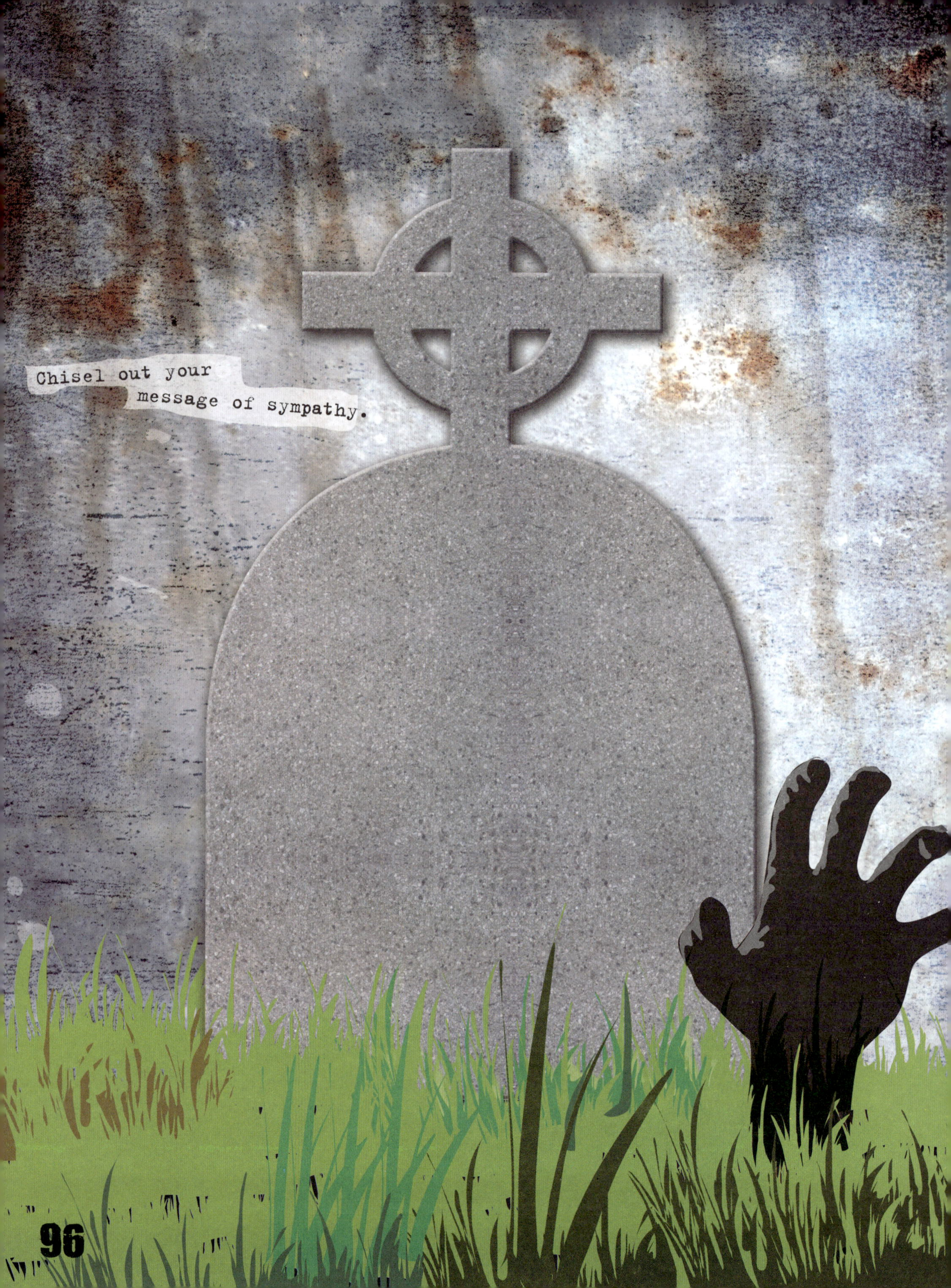
Chisel out your
message of sympathy.

Doodle and design
a zombie mouse pad.

ZOMBIE OF THE MONTH

Write your colleagues' names here.

The infection has spread to
your work.
Doodle your work colleagues as
gruesome hungry zombies!

Doodle in your friends
as freaky zombies
in this collection
of gory photos!

WORD SEARCH 5

d e c o m p o s e d l d
o d u w s u p e f o p e
m g s q t t i c e r r o
l g s f s r e k l a w t
n o t e y e b a l l o c
a l i t w f t s s d r s
u l d c t a h o s l m e
f r p o t c d c r f s p
e m s r o t t i n g n f
h o c p s i e h s e l f
s s o s t o g g a m t e
g w i e t n a c s s r s

corpse
decomposed
eyeball
flesh
flies
grotesque
maggots
putrefaction
rotting
stench
walkers
worms

Draw something
hideous here.

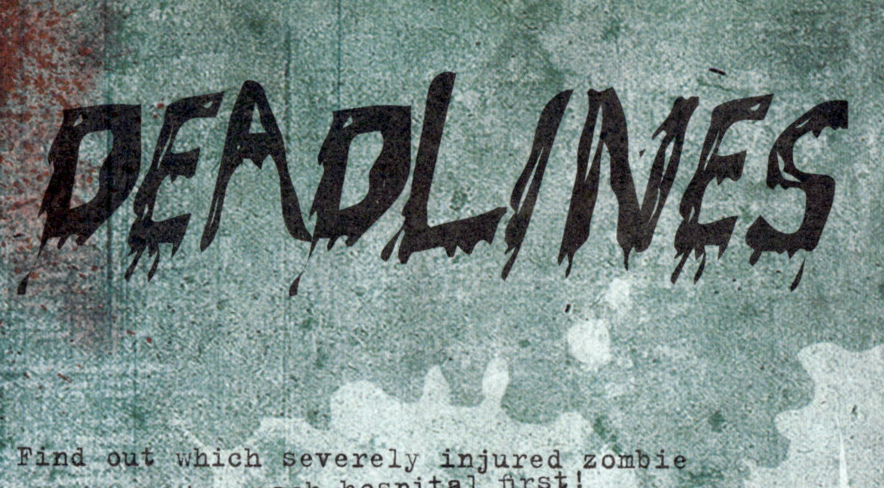

DEADLINES

Find out which severely injured zombie gets to reach hospital first!

Follow the mangled lines to see who will survive.

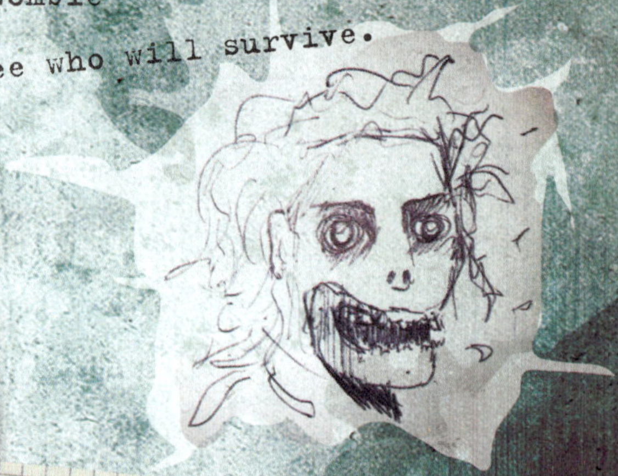

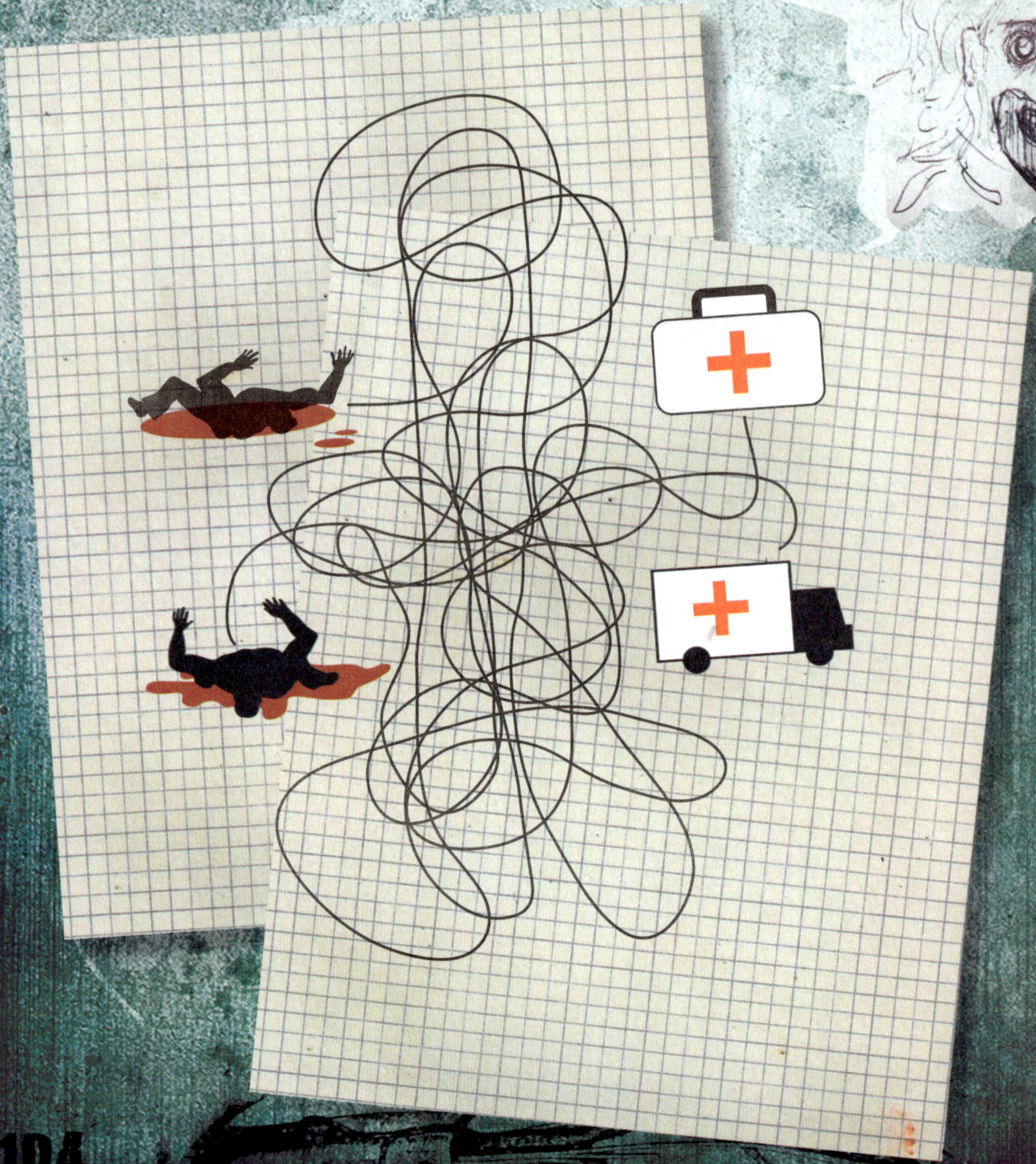

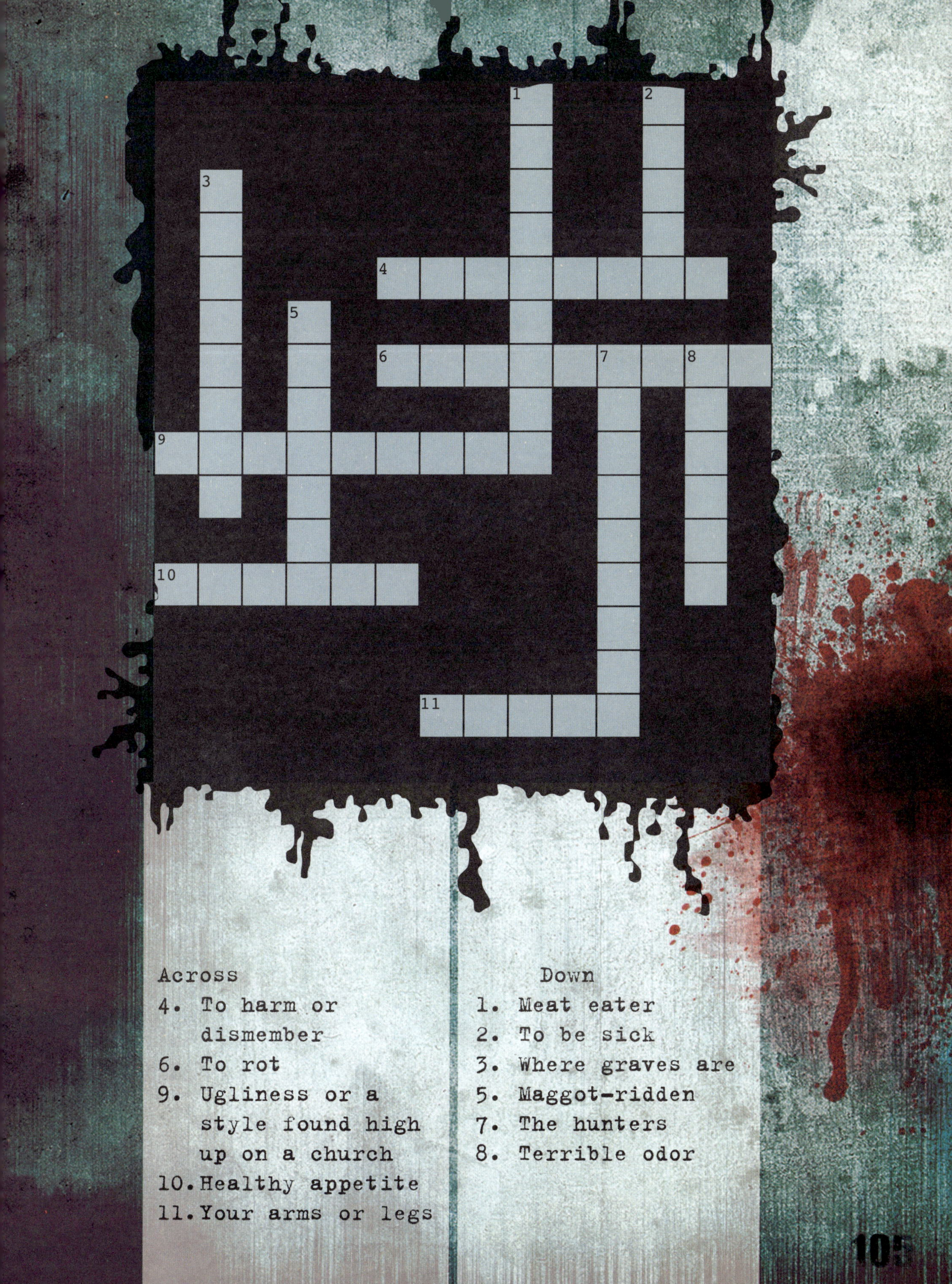

Across
4. To harm or dismember
6. To rot
9. Ugliness or a style found high up on a church
10. Healthy appetite
11. Your arms or legs

Down
1. Meat eater
2. To be sick
3. Where graves are
5. Maggot-ridden
7. The hunters
8. Terrible odor

ZOMBIE HANGMAN

Cross off the dead letters.

ABCDEFGHIJKLMNOPQRSTUVWXYZ

Draw your hangman.

Enter your blood-soaked words here.

ABCDEFG
HIJKLM
NOPQRST
UVWXYZ

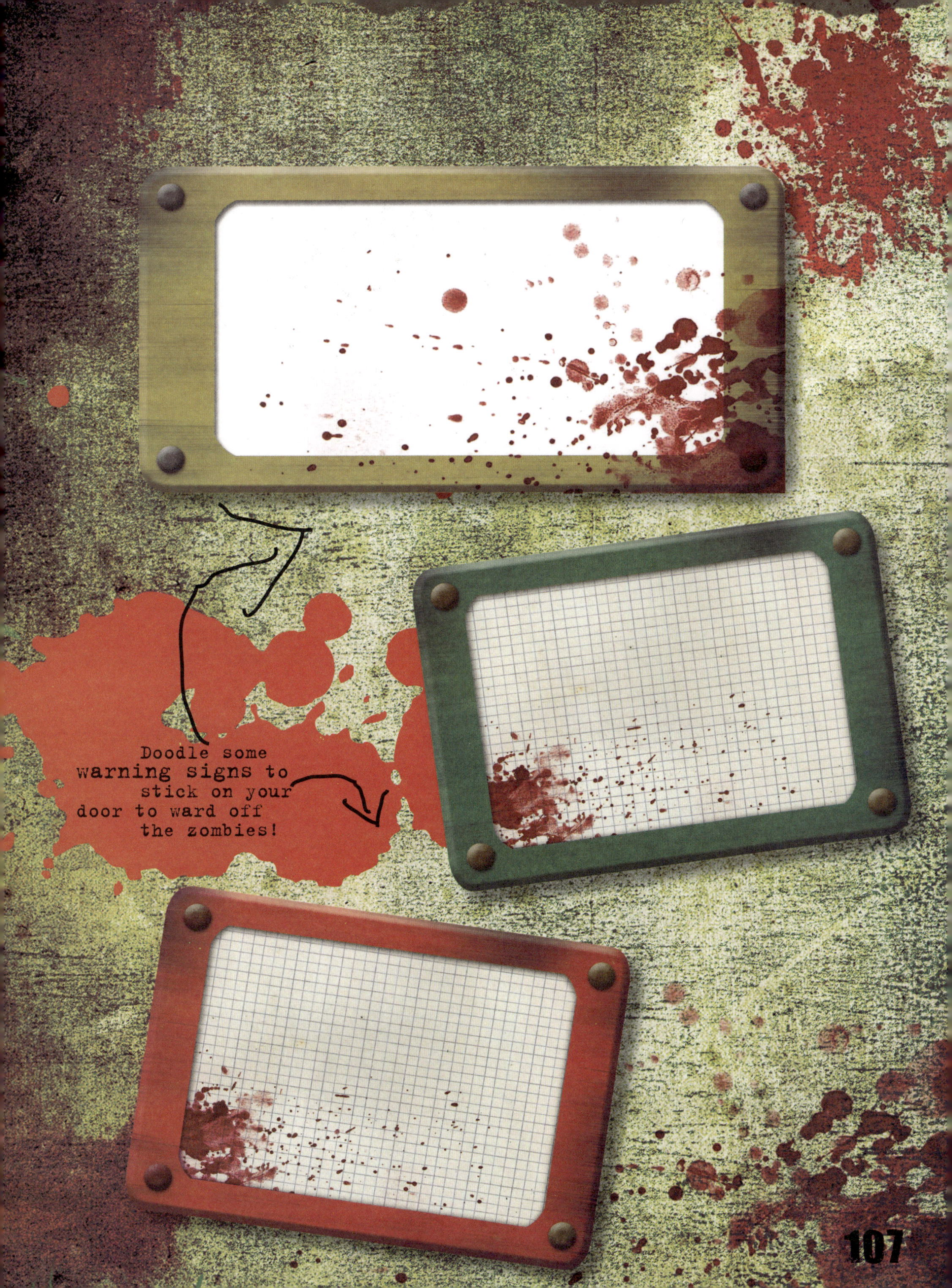

Doodle some
warning signs to
stick on your
door to ward off
the zombies!

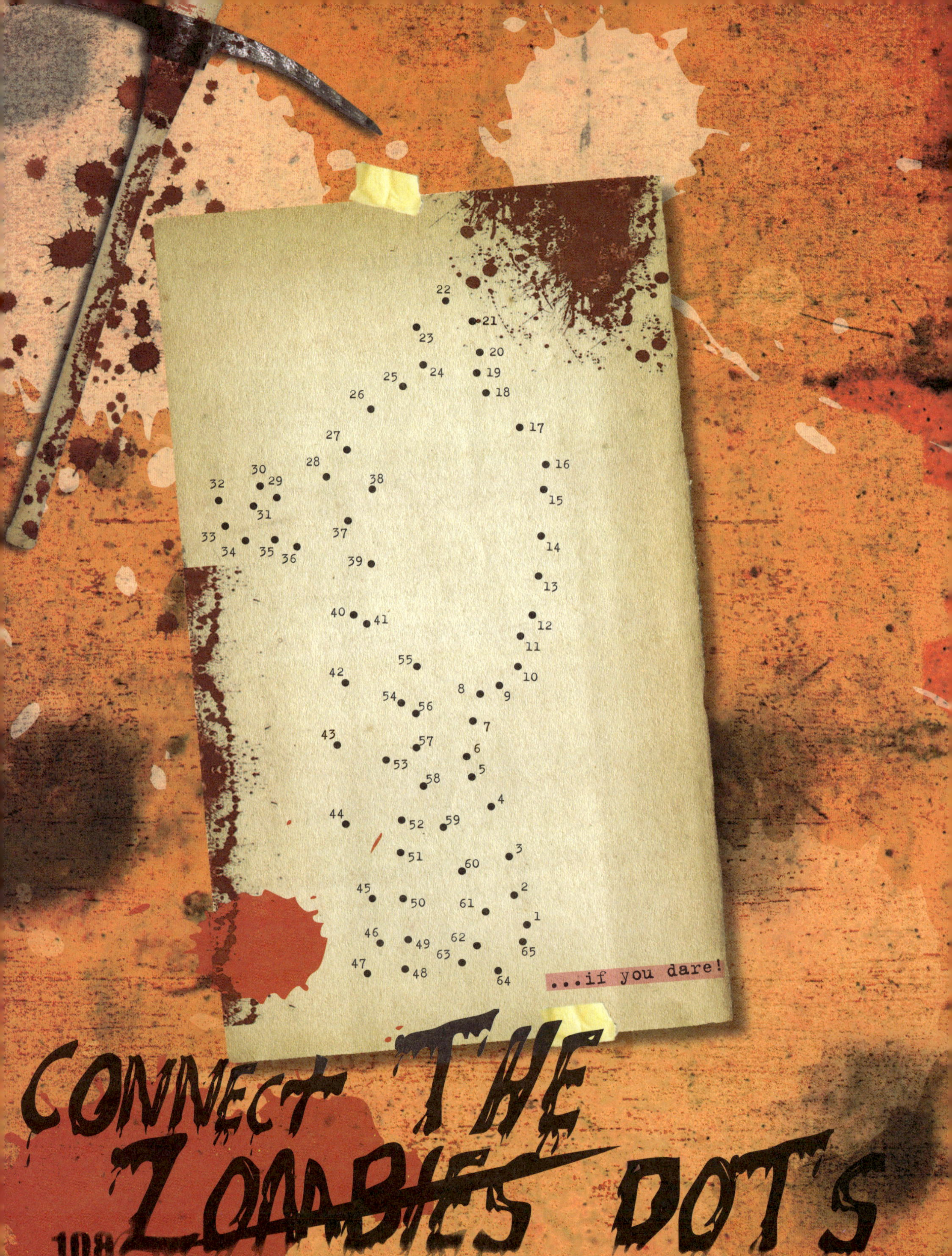
...if you dare!
CONNECT THE
ZOMBIES DOTS

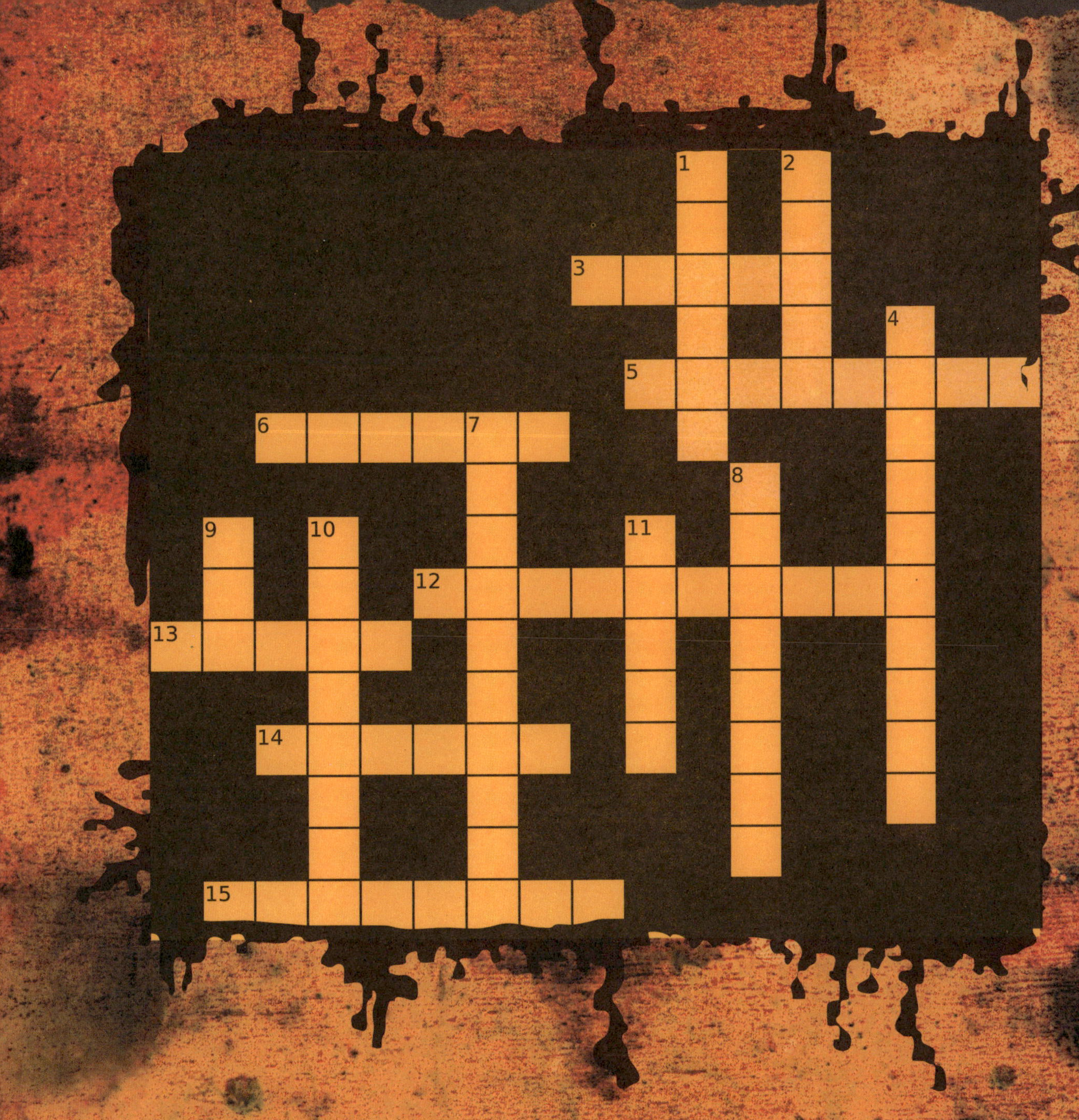

Across

3. Tool for digging
5. One who kills
6. The walking dead
12. To behead
13. A gathering to consume
14. A wooden box
15. Power tool for cutting

Down

1. Widespread disease
2. When you get cut you ________
4. End of the world
7. Part of your digestive system
8. Another word for intestines
9. To chop wood with
10. a nightmare future
11. your back bone

Doodle your zombie designs onto this template to customize your funky underwear.

practice

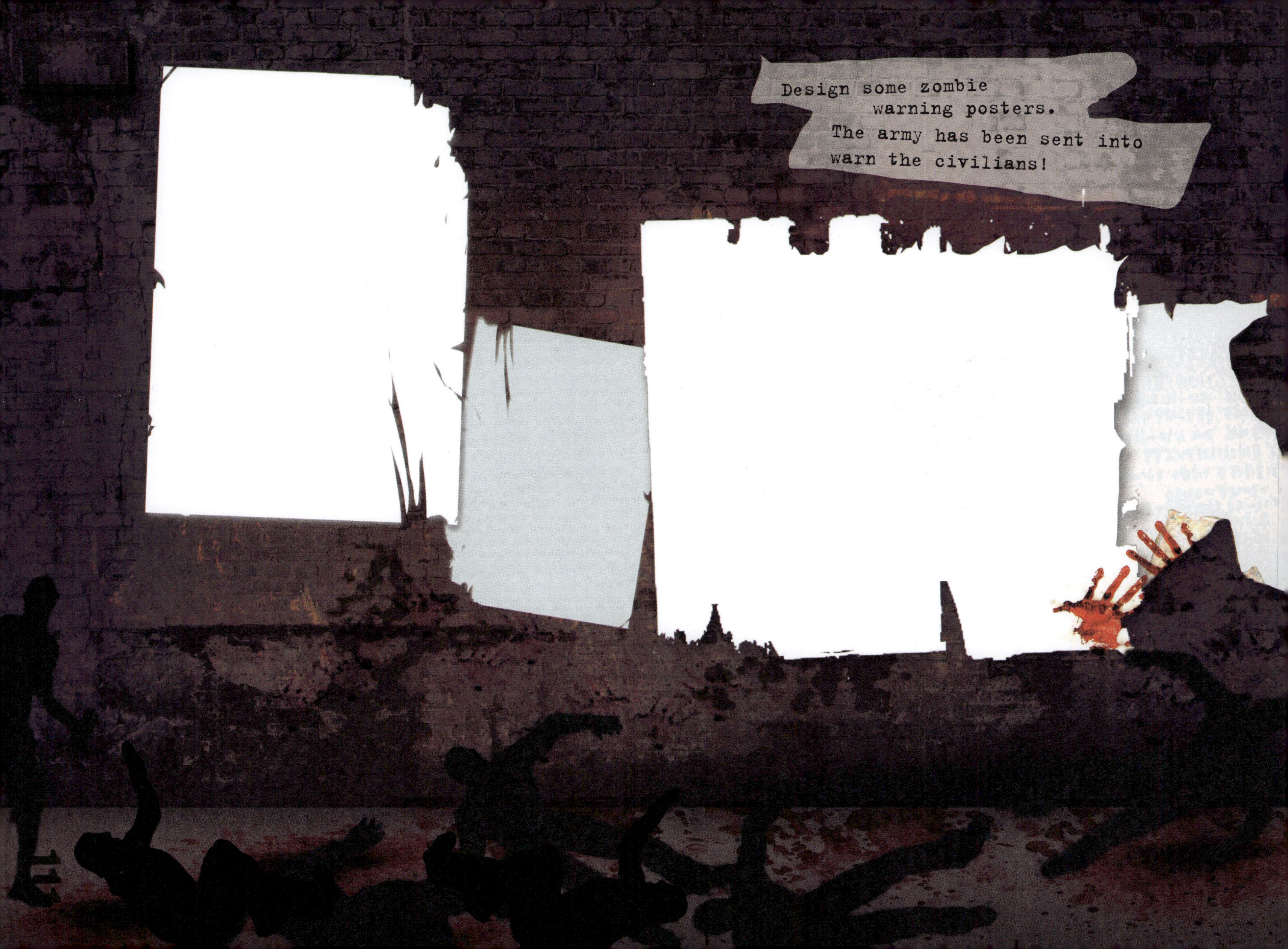
Design some zombie
warning posters.
The army has been sent into
warn the civilians!

Doodle and design
a zombie mouse pad.

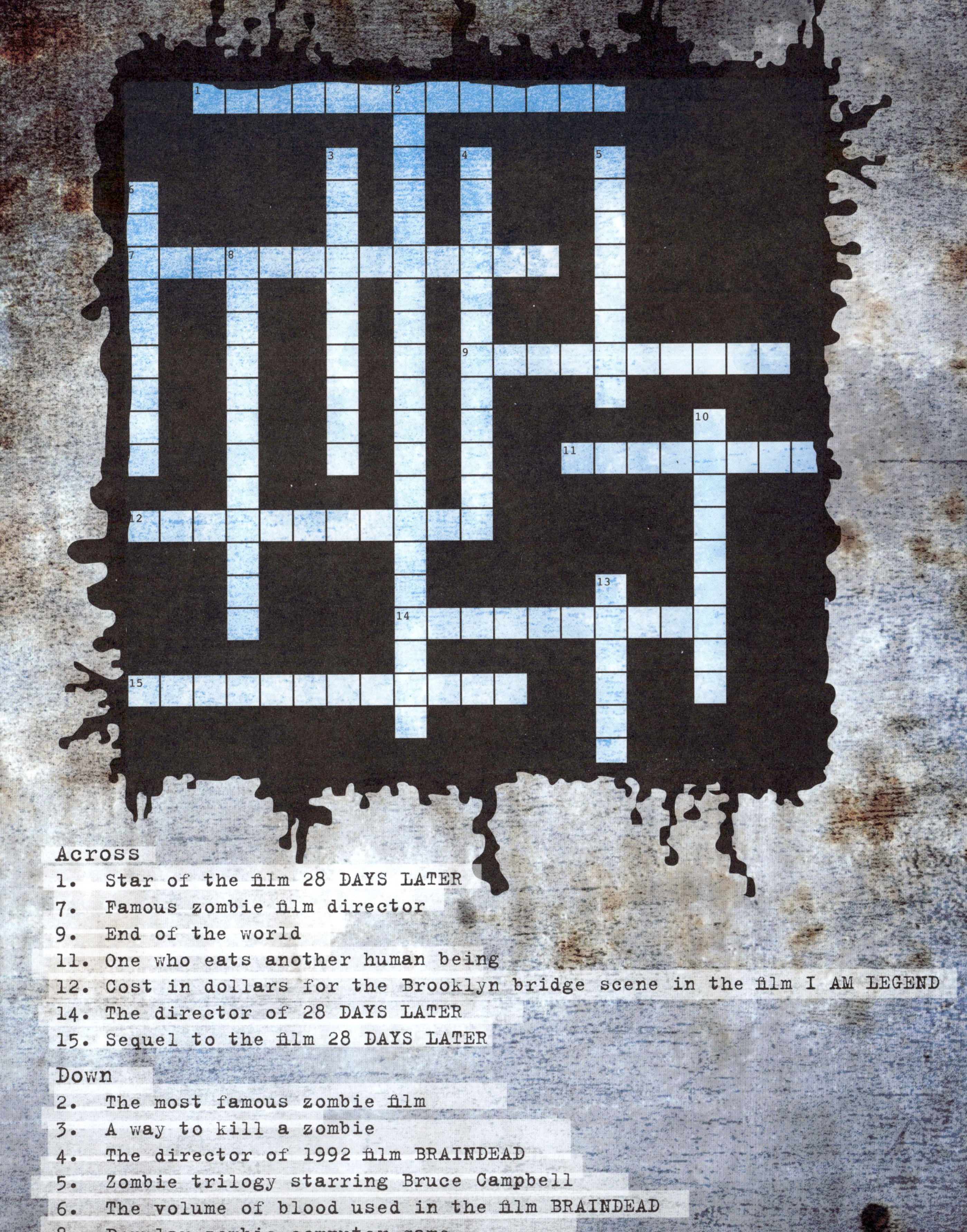

Across
1. Star of the film 28 DAYS LATER
7. Famous zombie film director
9. End of the world
11. One who eats another human being
12. Cost in dollars for the Brooklyn bridge scene in the film I AM LEGEND
14. The director of 28 DAYS LATER
15. Sequel to the film 28 DAYS LATER

Down
2. The most famous zombie film
3. A way to kill a zombie
4. The director of 1992 film BRAINDEAD
5. Zombie trilogy starring Bruce Campbell
6. The volume of blood used in the film BRAINDEAD
8. Popular zombie computer game
10. The star of the film SHAUN OF THE DEAD
13. A place to keep dead bodies before burial

TOP TEN LISTS

IN SHAUN OF THE DEAD, WHEN SHAUN TELLS ED NOT TO SAY ZOMBIE ("THE ZED WORD!"), ITS AN HOMAGE TO THE FACT THE WORD ZOMBIE THAT WAS NEVER USED IN MOST OF GEORGE A. ROMEROS FILMS.

Top ten best zombie films

Top ten worst zombie films

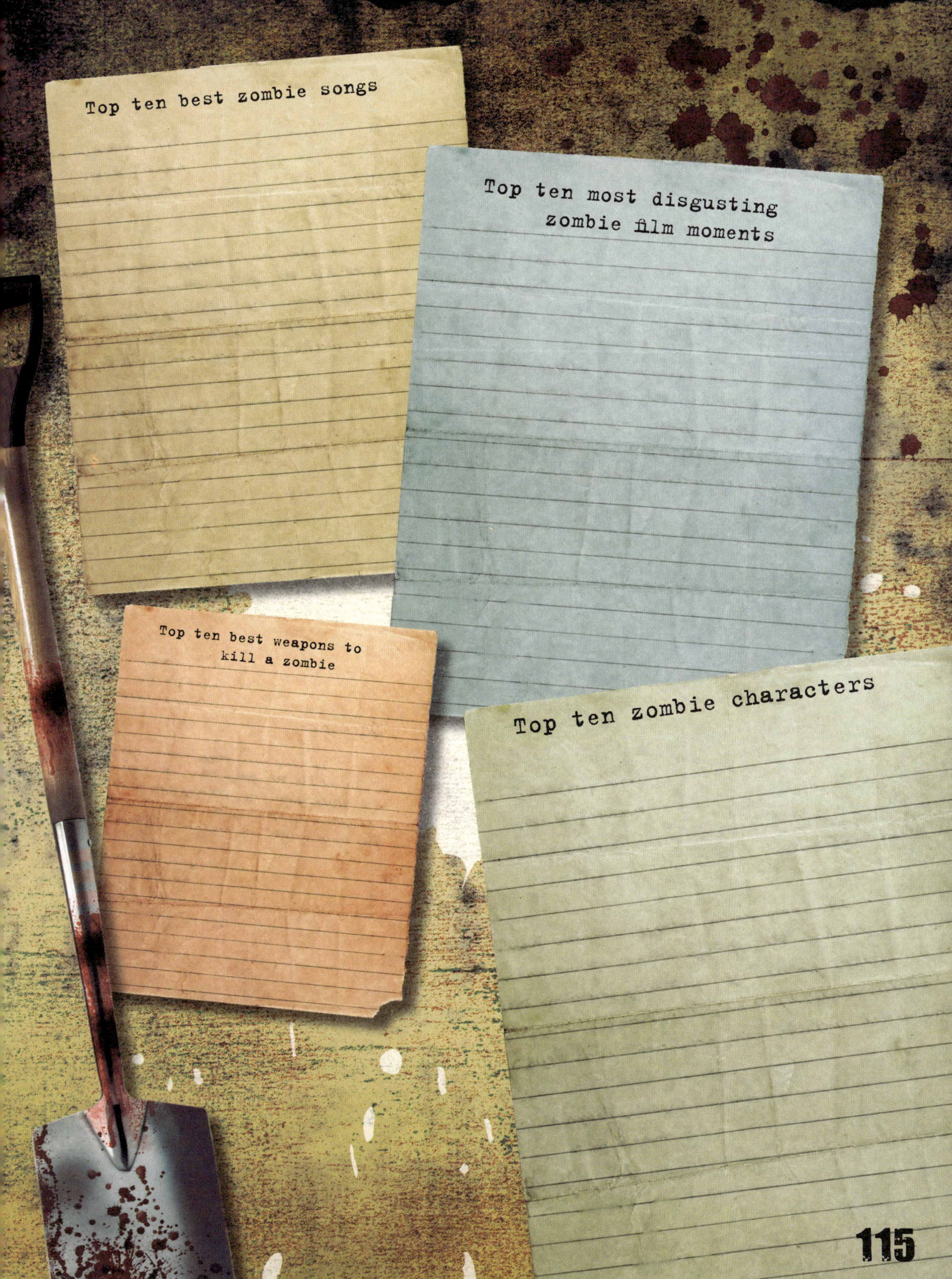
Top ten best zombie songs
Top ten most disgusting zombie film moments
Top ten best weapons to kill a zombie
Top ten zombie characters

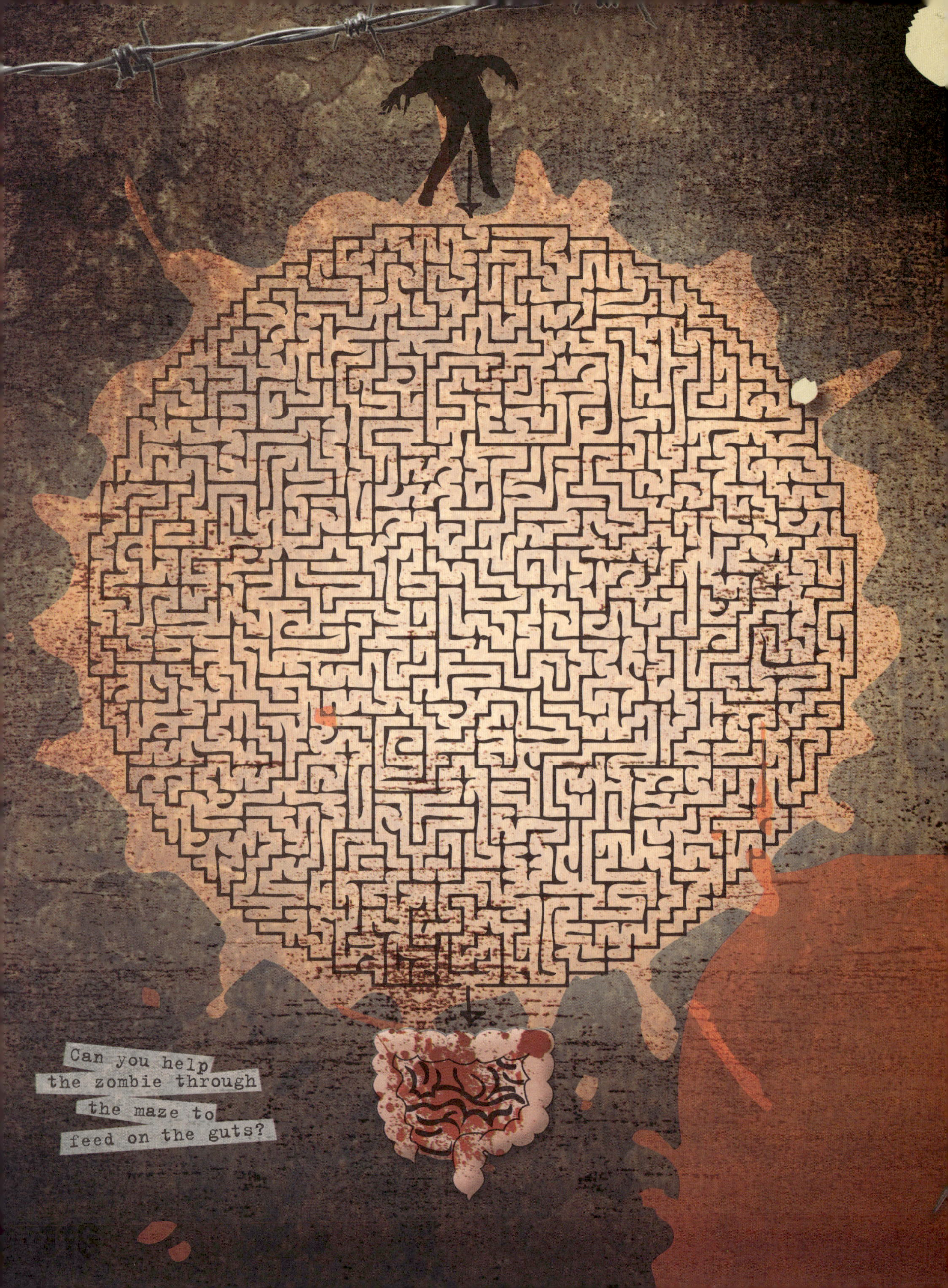
Can you help
the zombie through
the maze to
feed on the guts?

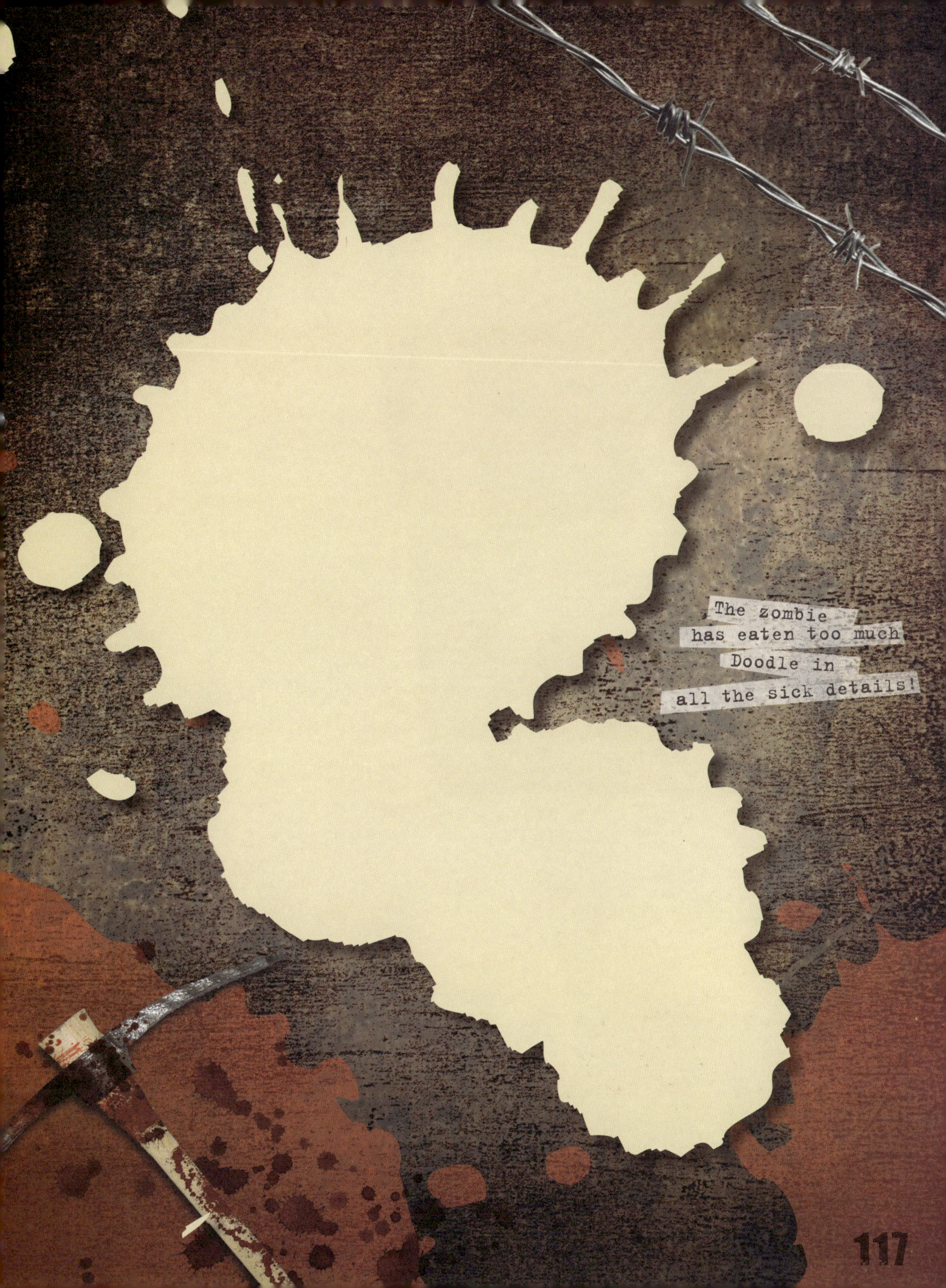
The zombie
has eaten too much.
Doodle in
all the sick details!

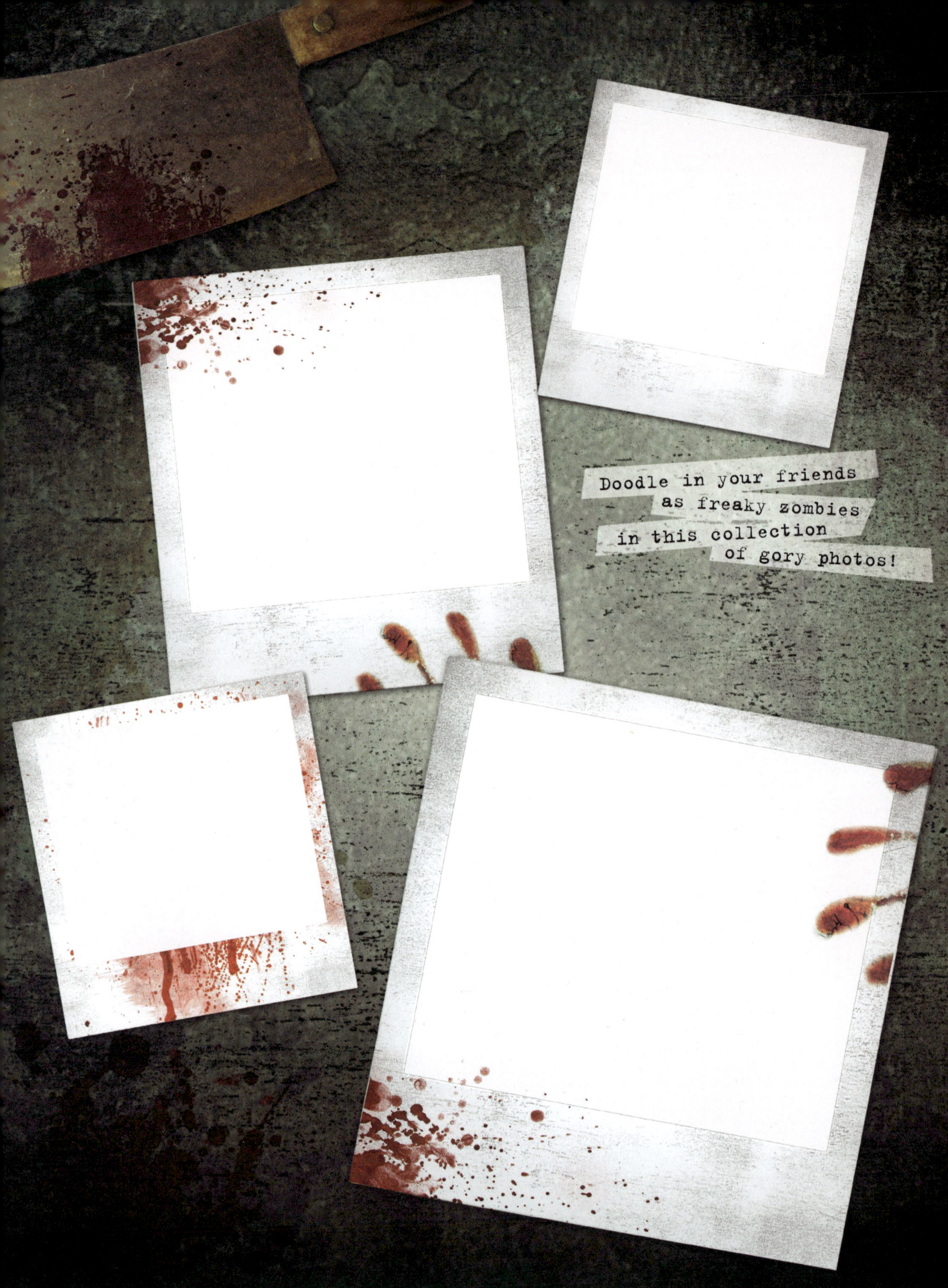
Doodle in your friends
as freaky zombies
in this collection
of gory photos!

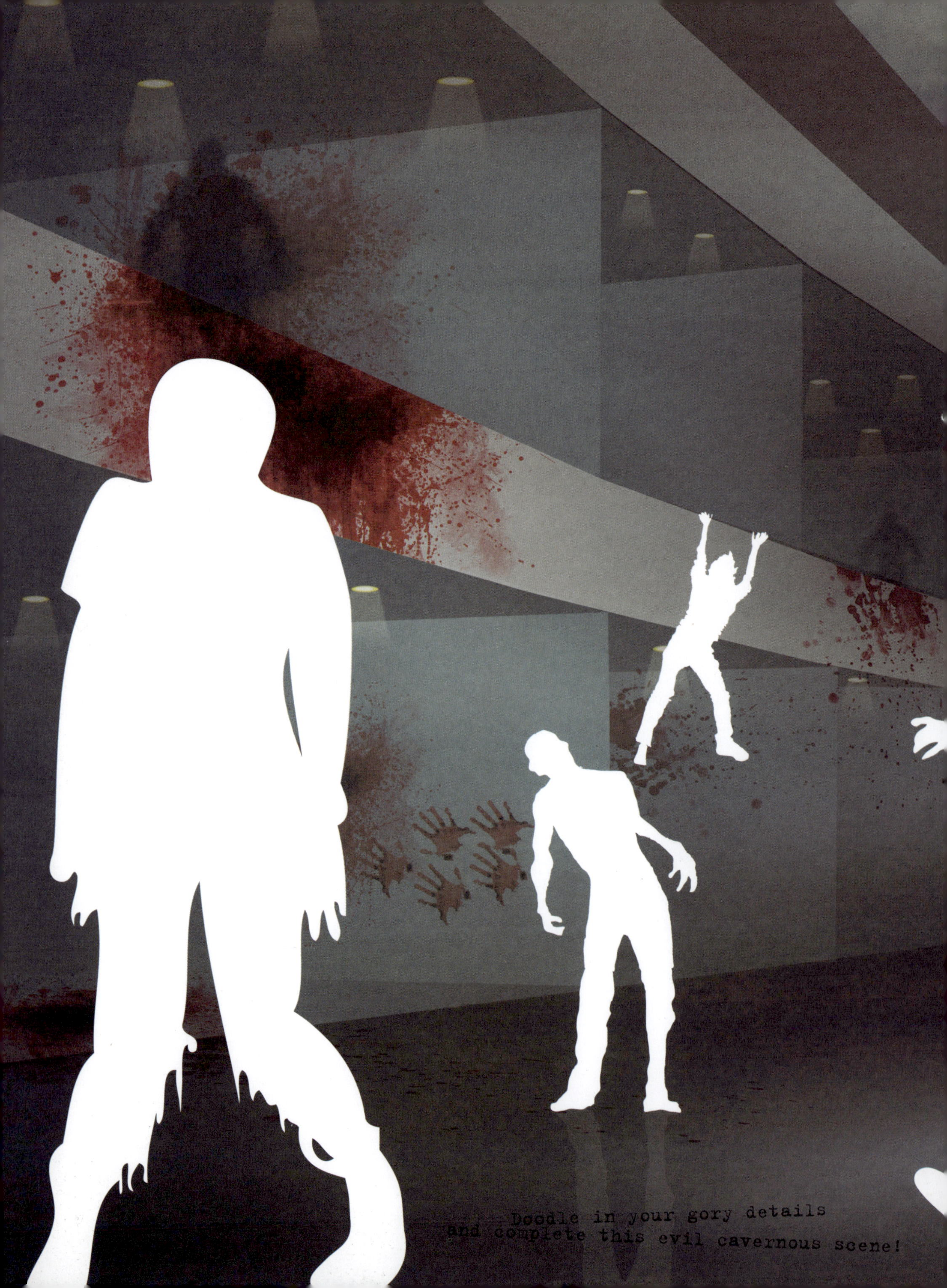

Doodle in your gory details
and complete this evil cavernous scene!

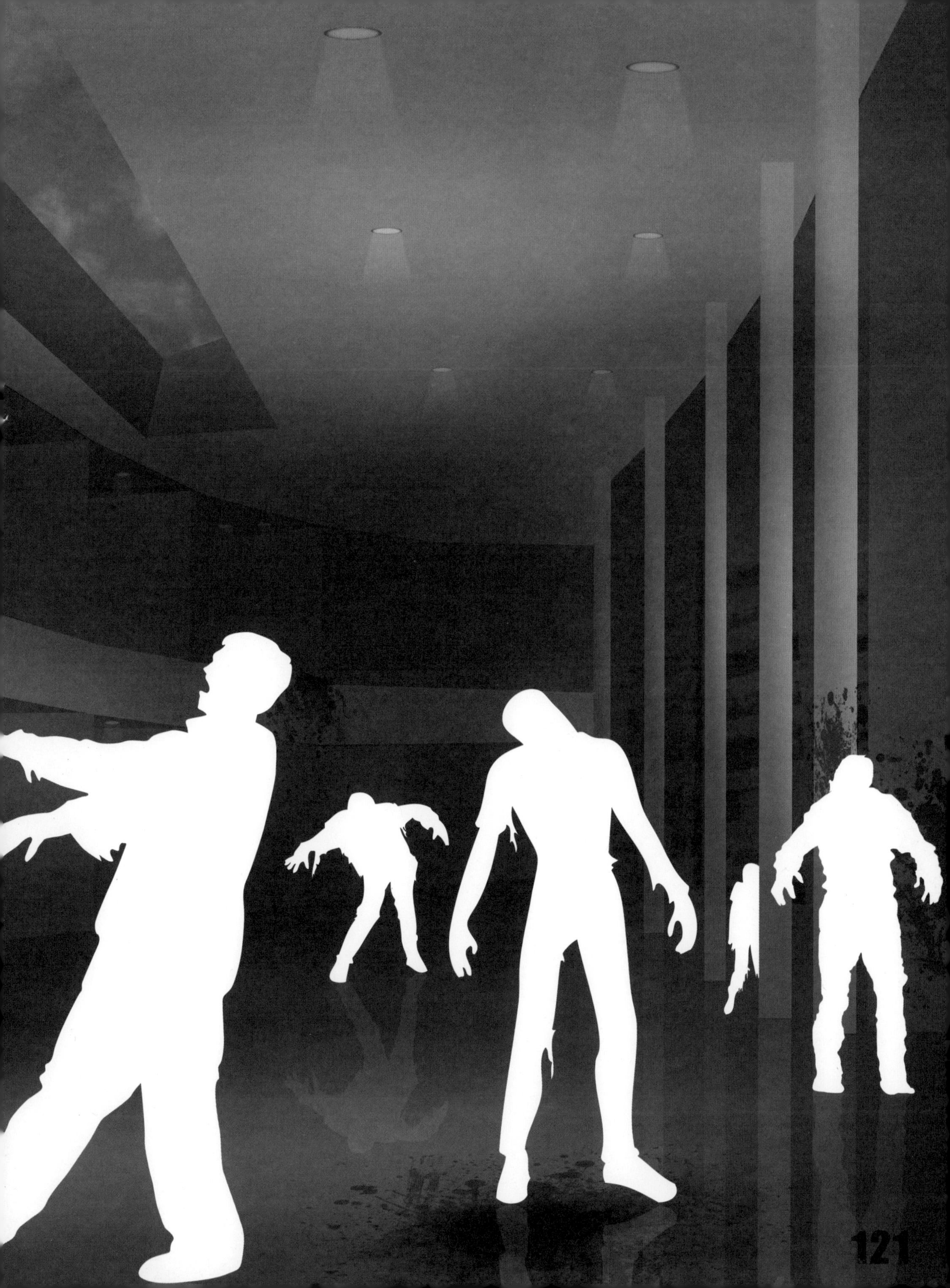

Design some party name tags for your guests. Customize with fun questions!

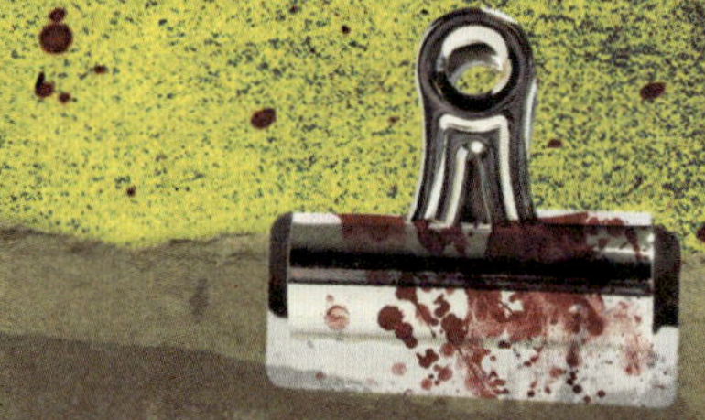

KARL´S KILLER PARTY

name: Isack Brains

Worst zombie film: None of them!

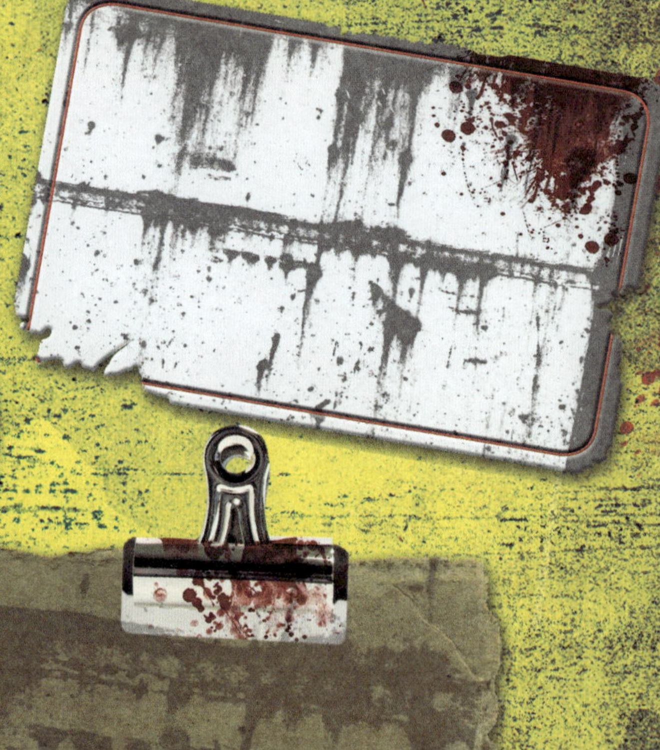

example

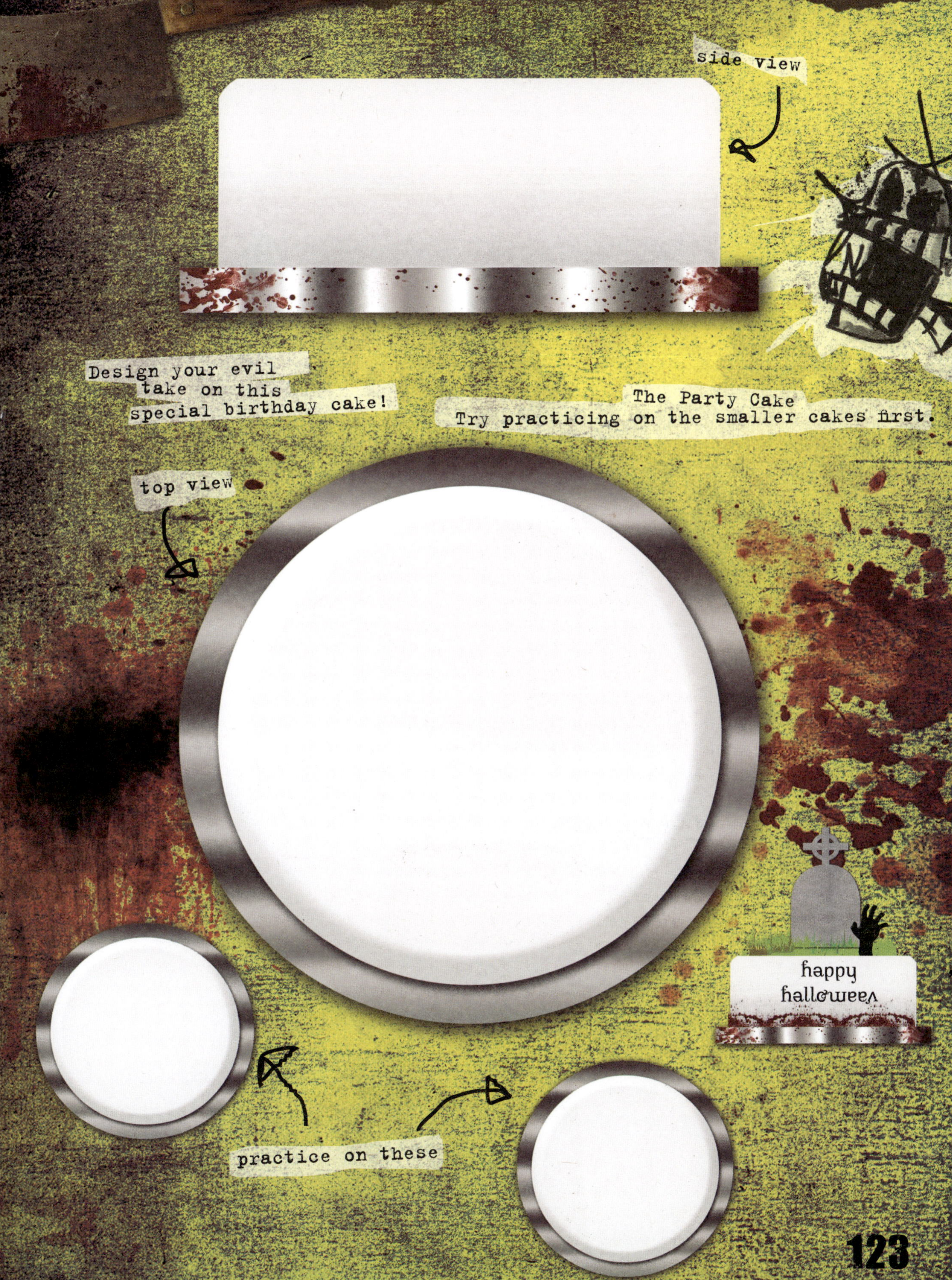
side view
Design your evil
take on this
special birthday cake!
The Party Cake
Try practicing on the smaller cakes first.
top view
happy
halloween
practice on these

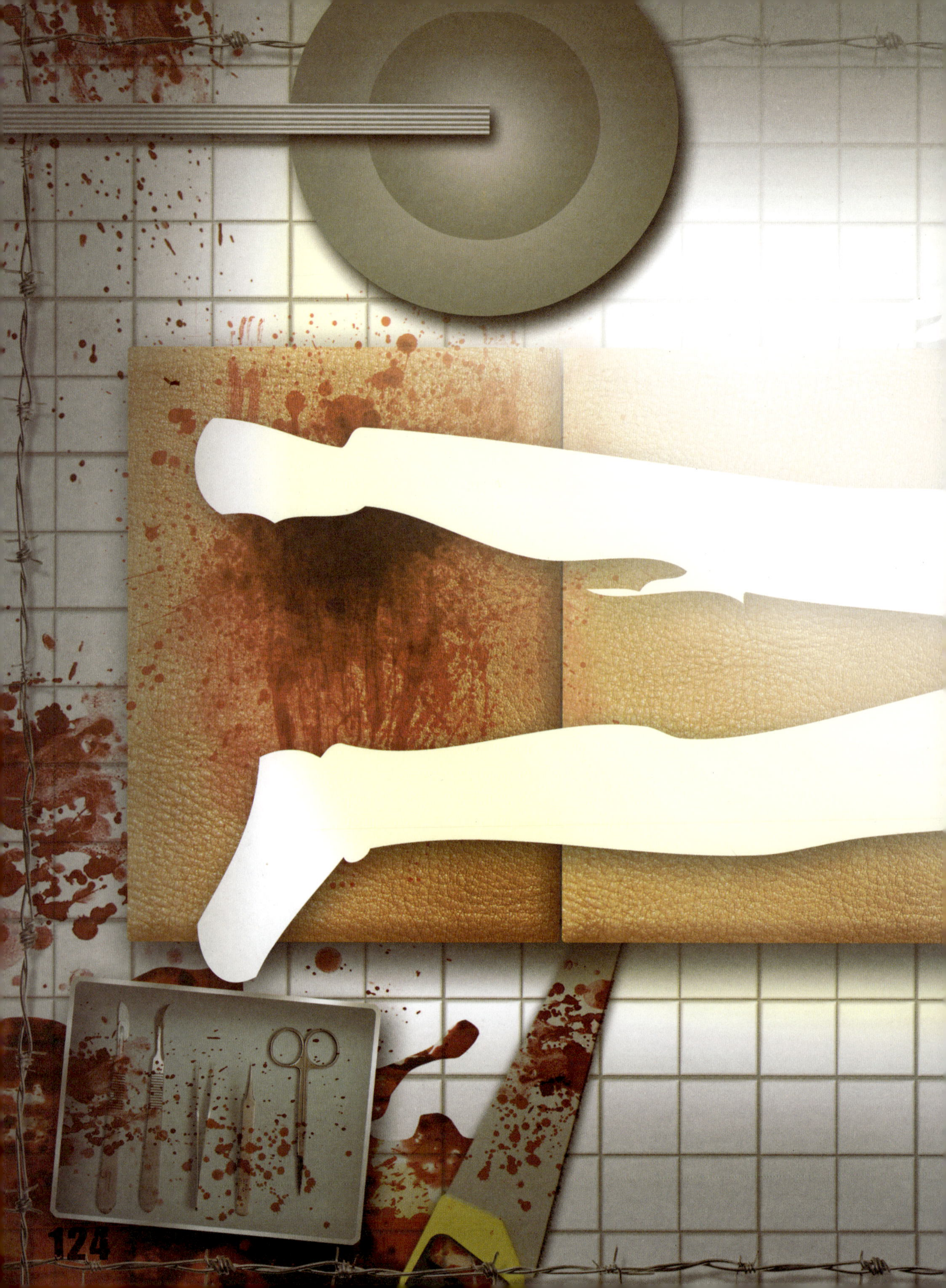

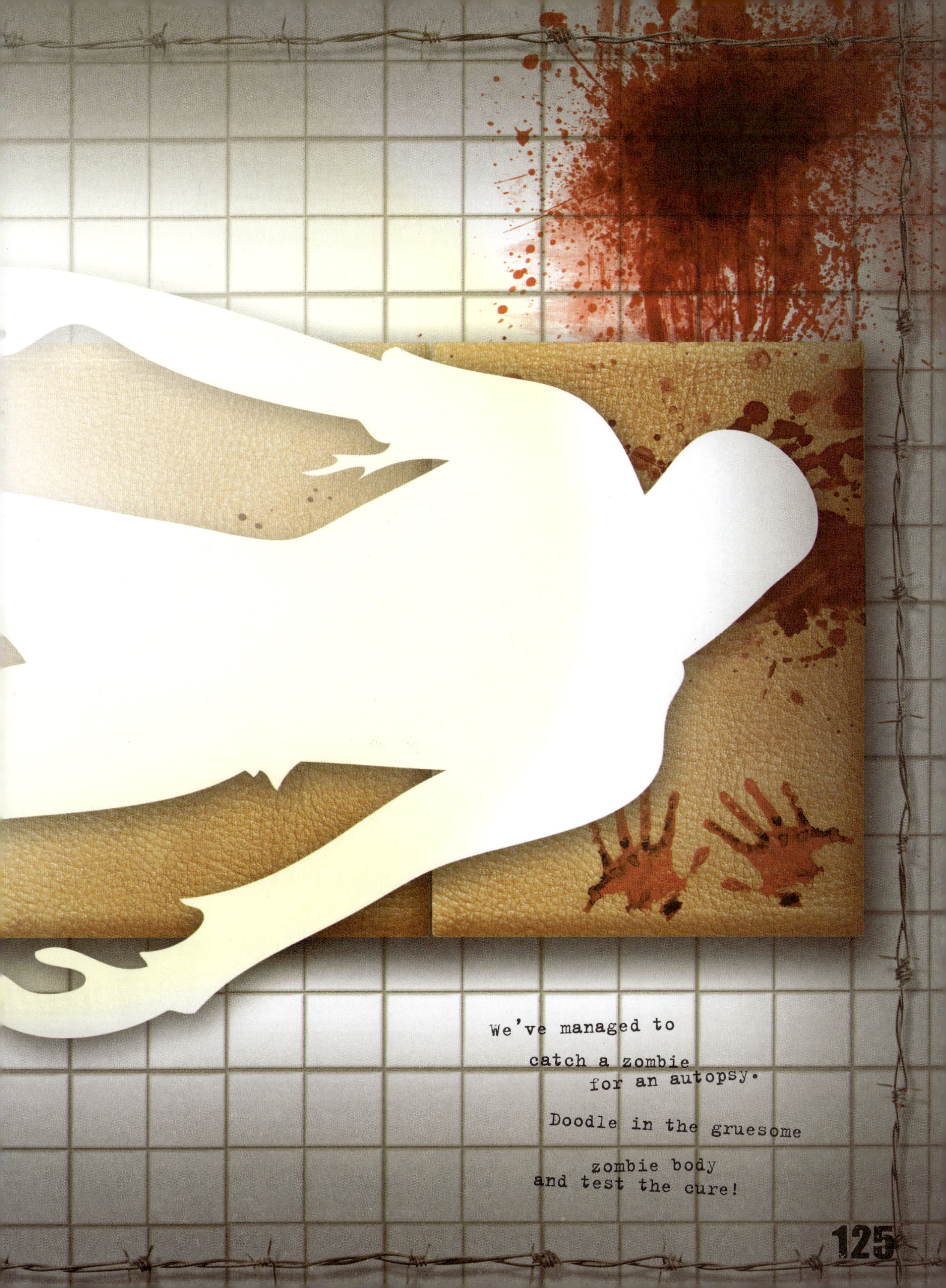

We've managed to

catch a zombie
for an autopsy.

Doodle in the gruesome

zombie body
and test the cure!

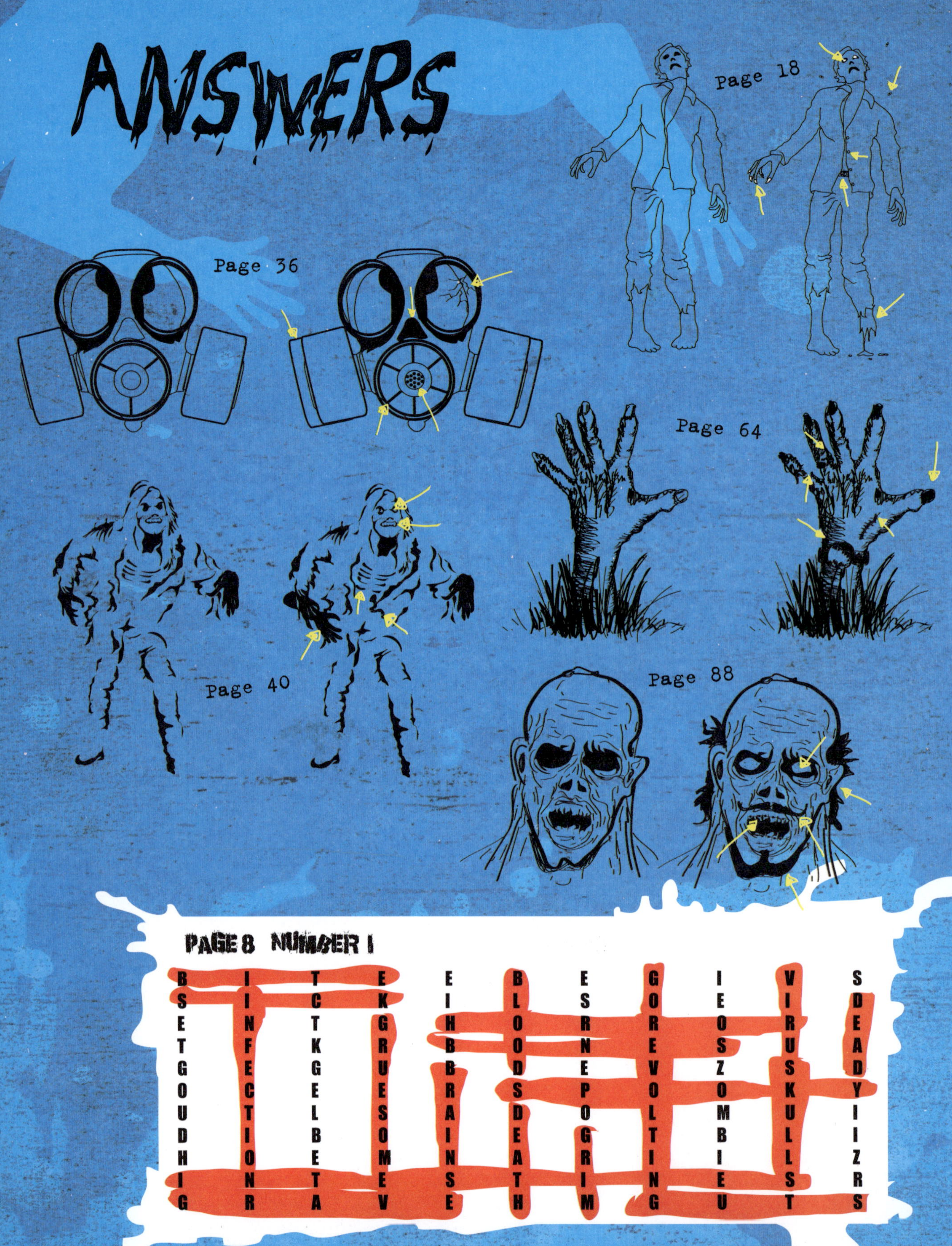
ANSWERS
Page 18
Page 36
Page 64
Page 40
Page 88
PAGE 8 NUMBER 1
B I T E E B E G I V S
S I C K I L S O E I D
E N T G H O R R O R E
T F K R B O N E S U A
G E G U B D E V Z S D
O C E E R S P O O K Y
U T L S A D O L M U I
D I B O I E G T B L I
H O E M N A R I I L Z
I N T E S T I N E S R
G R A V E H M G U T S

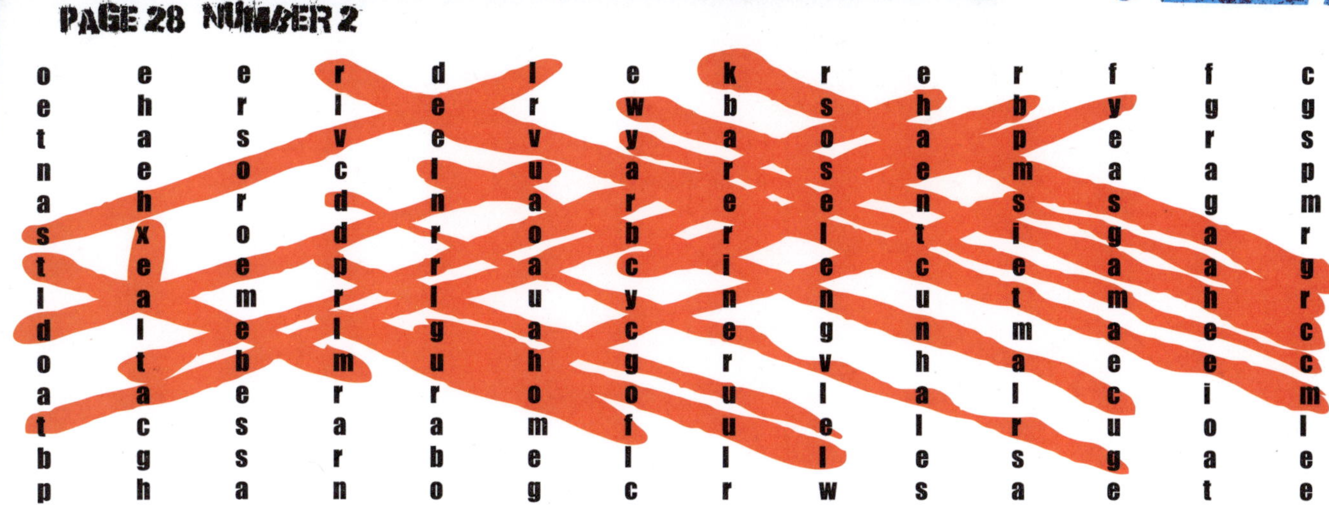

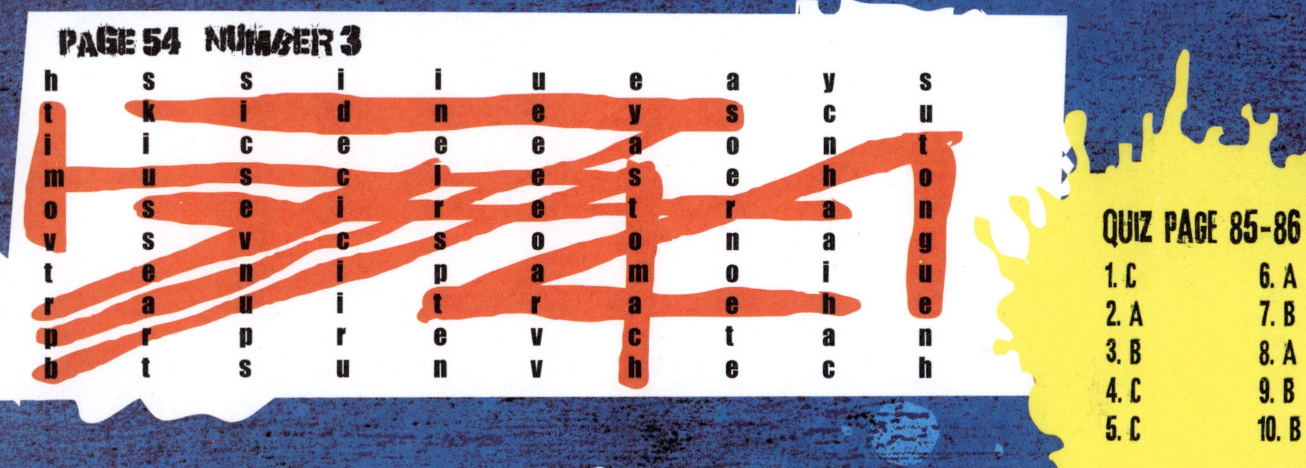

QUIZ PAGE 85-86

1. C	6. A
2. A	7. B
3. B	8. A
4. C	9. B
5. C	10. B

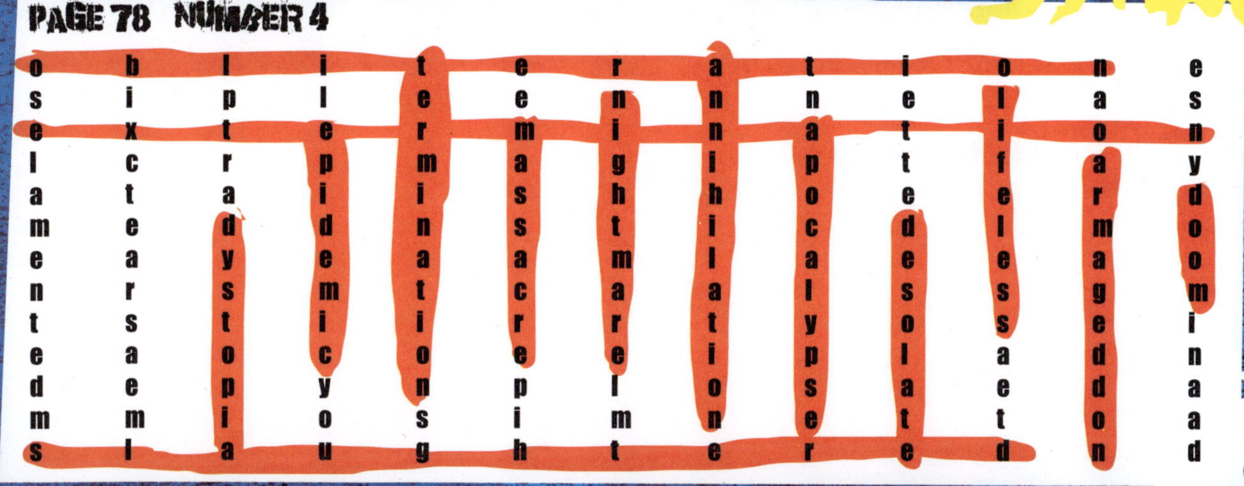

PAGE 102 NUMBER 5

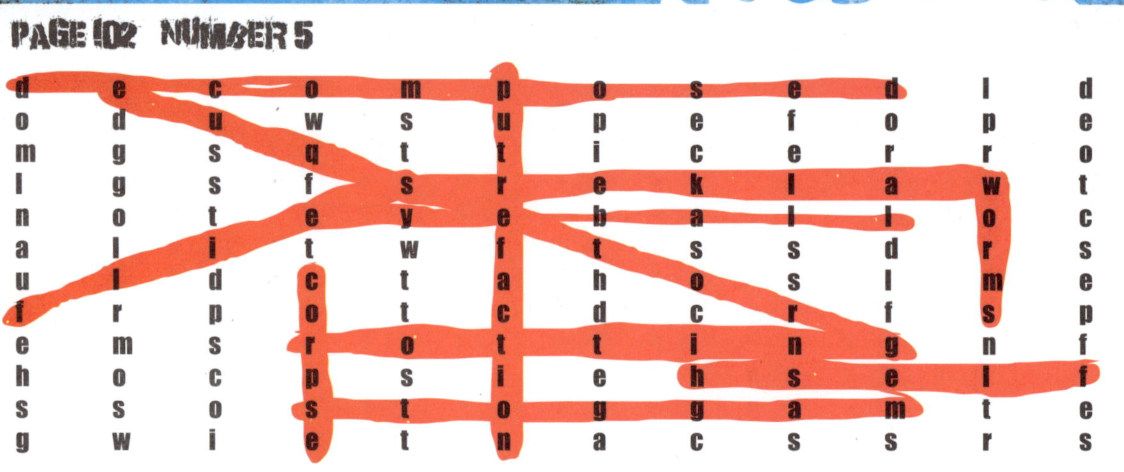

PAGE 113

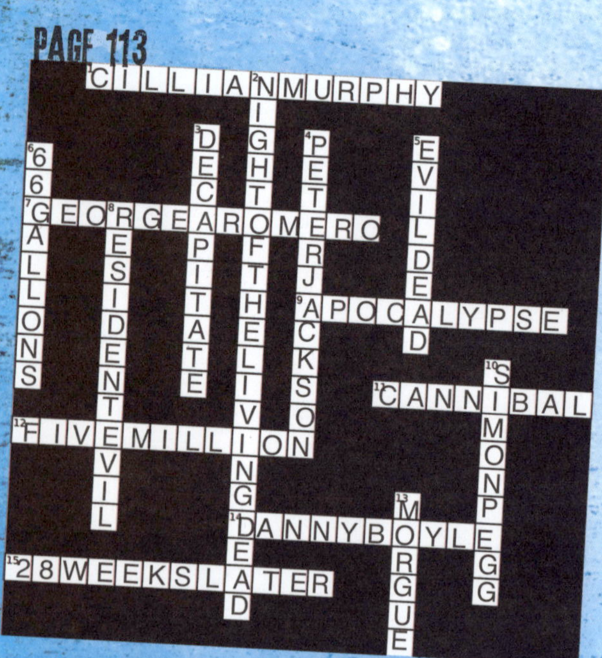

PAGE 109

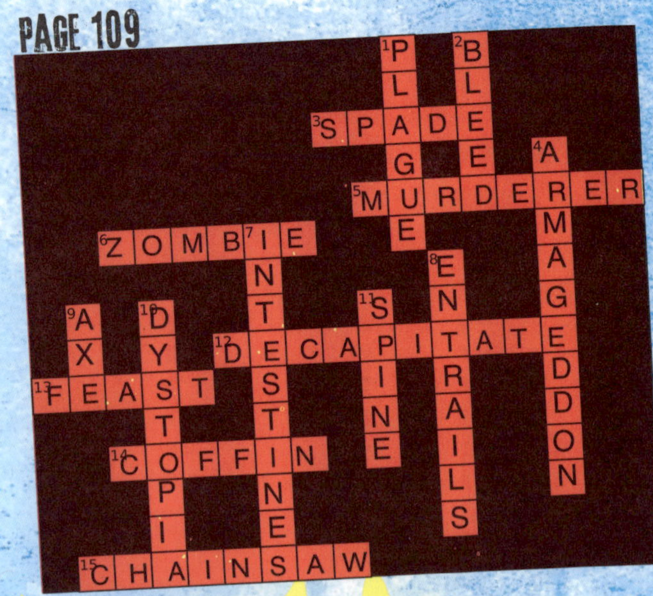

PAGE 105

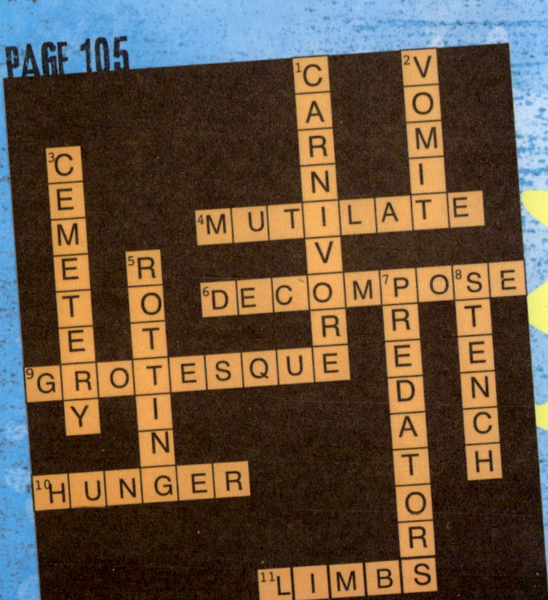

PAGE 116

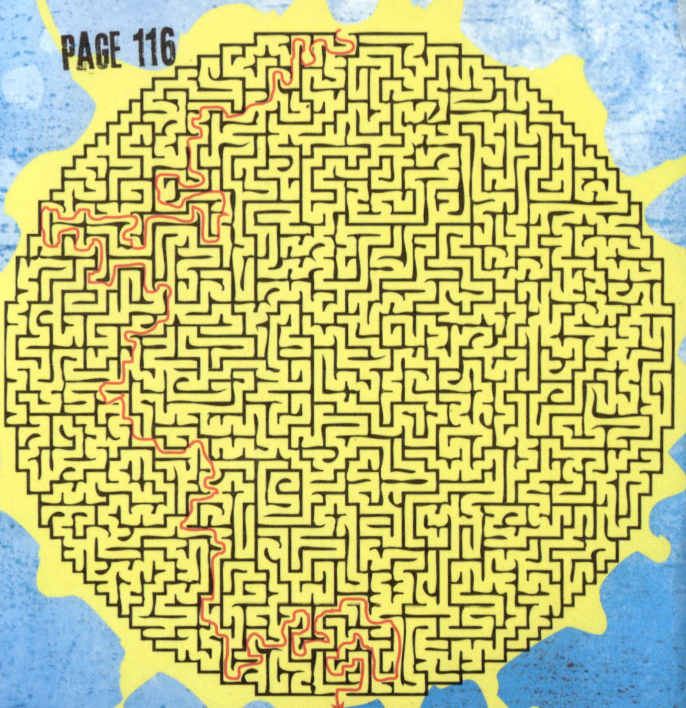